THE ETHICS OF LEGAL COERCION

PHILOSOPHICAL STUDIES SERIES
IN PHILOSOPHY

VOLUME 26

JOHN D. HODSON

Department of Philosophy, The University of Texas at Austin

THE ETHICS
OF LEGAL COERCION

D. REIDEL PUBLISHING COMPANY

DORDRECHT : HOLLAND / BOSTON : U.S.A.

LONDON : ENGLAND

Library of Congress Cataloging in Publication Data

Hodson, John D., 1948–
    The ethics of legal coercion.

    (Philosophical studies series in philosophy; v. 26)
    Bibliography: p.
    Includes indexes.
    1. Law–Philosophy.   2.   Law and ethics.   I.   Title.
II.   Series.
K250.H63   1983   340′.112   83-3296
ISBN 90–277–1494–0

Published by D. Reidel Publishing Company,
P.O. Box 17, 3300 AA Dordrecht, Holland.

Sold and distributed in the U.S.A. and Canada
by Kluwer Boston Inc.,
190 Old Derby Street, Hingham, MA 02043, U.S.A.

In all other countries, sold and distributed
by Kluwer Academic Publishers Group,
P.O. Box 322, 3300 AH Dordrecht, Holland.

D. Reidel Publishing Company is a member of the Kluwer Group.

Printed in The Netherlands.

For Shelagh

TABLE OF CONTENTS

ACKNOWLEDGEMENTS

In completing the present work, I have accumulated a number of debts, and I hope at least to acknowledge them here, since some could never be repaid.

I have relied heavily on the research resources of the University of Texas at Austin. This has included financial assistance from the University of Texas Research Institute. Also, some of my work on this project has been supported by a Summer Stipend from the National Endowment for the Humanities.

Small portions of this work have made prior public appearances. A part of Chapter Four appeared in 'The Principle of Paternalism', *American Philosophical Quarterly* 14 (January, 1977), pp. 61–69. It is included here by permission. Some of Chapter Four also made an appearance as part of my Ph.D. dissertation, completed at the University of Arizona in 1976. A portion of Chapter Five, approximately equivalent to Sections 5.2 and 5.3, was presented in 1978 at the Western Division meetings of the American Philosophical Association under the title 'Rights to Assistance'.

I would also like to acknowledge a debt to the philosophical work of Joel Feinberg, whose writings so often define the issues in this field and point the way to their resolution. My own efforts in this area certainly would have been much poorer had he not cleared so much of the path before me.

Several persons have offered valuable comments on earlier drafts of work presented here. Thanks are owed to Don Hubin, Chuck Carr, Raymond Martin, Richard Wasserstrom, Carl Cohen, Donald VanDeVeer, Edmund Pincoffs, and members of the philosophy and law discussion group at the University of Texas at Austin.

Although nearly all of this book was written after I completed my graduate work, it nonetheless reflects what I gained from that experience. I would like to thank my professors at the University of Arizona, as well as fellow graduate students of my era, for providing a very rewarding experience. Special thanks are owed, first, to Ronald D. Milo, who, among other things, guided me through the intricacies of metaethical theory. While such issues are not taken up here, they provide an important background for the ones that are.

My greatest philosophical debt is to Jeffrie G. Murphy, who directed my dissertation and under whose tutelage I first seriously studied the issues examined in this book. I am grateful to him for that, as well as for continued advice, assistance, and encouragement in the years since I completed my graduate work.

Finally, I would like to thank my wife Shelagh for help with matters of grammar and style, for tolerating my preoccupation with this project, and simply for being there. I dedicate this book to her.

Needless to say, I have reserved the right to make my own mistakes despite the contributions of those mentioned above.

J. D. H.

INTRODUCTION

Are all of the commonly accepted aims of the use of law justifiable? Which kinds of behavior are justifiably prohibited, which kinds justifiably required? What uses of law are not defensible? How can the legitimacy or the illegitimacy of various uses of law be explained or accounted for? These are questions the answering of which involves one in many issues of moral principle, for the answers require that one adopt positions — even if only implicitly — on further questions of what kinds of actions or policies are morally or ethically acceptable. The present work, aimed at questions of these kinds, is thus a study in the ethical evaluation of major uses of legal coercion. It is an attempt to provide a framework within which many questions about the proper uses of law may be fruitfully discussed. The framework, if successful, can be used by anyone asking questions about the defensibility of particular or general uses of law, whether from the perspective of someone considering whether to bring about some new legal provision, from the perspective of someone concerned to evaluate an existing provision, or from that of someone concerned more abstractly with questions about the appropriate substance of an ideal legal system.

In addressing these and associated issues, I shall be exploring the extent to which an ethics based on respect for persons and their autonomy can handle satisfactorily the problems arising here. Over the past century or two, utilitarian thinking has tended to dominate discussion of these issues. The problem of ethical limits to the kinds of legislation which may be enacted is frequently (and appropriately) discussed in the terms generated by John Stuart Mill's work in *On Liberty* (1859), and that calls for assessment of the professedly utilitarian foundation of Mill's position. Even recent disscussion of these matters is sufficiently utilitarian for one commentator to have found it possible to describe the debate concerning them as an "in-house quarrel among utilitarians".[1] Utilitarians would have it that legislation, as well as the actions of individuals, should be evaluated ultimately only in terms of the effects of the legislation or the actions on the happiness, pleasure, or satisfactions of human beings (or all sentient beings). Only that which in some way maximizes these desired results is acceptable to the utilitarian. One aim of the present work is to show how a non-utilitarian approach can provide useful insights into the theory of the proper uses of law.

It is certainly true that the past decade has seen some major philosophical works which share not only a non-utiliatrian perspective, but also, roughly speaking, a 'respect-for-persons' perspective.[2] While this is not the place to give a critique of these works, I do want to suggest that none supplants the need for further non-utilitarian treatment of the problems of normative legal philosophy. No comprehensive discussion of various uses of law has been undertaken from a non-utilitarian viewpoint. Theorists have taken positions on the legitimacy of certain uses of law, and in some cases the basis for the positions has been well-explained. However, a unified respect-for-persons treatment which discusses the various more specific issues in the field and explains how certain positions express that viewpoint better than others has not been available. The present study is designed to help fill this gap.

I shall do little to defend my selection of a commitment to the moral importance of persons as a normative foundation. It seems to me that some principle expressing such a commitment must be postulated if we are to account for widely shared considered convictions on various moral issues. Many well-known examples are designed to show that utilitarianism fails on this score, for instance, because it cannot provide any objection in principle to the sacrificing of an innocent minority for the sake of the greater satisfaction of a majority. Utilitarian responses to this sort of objection do not seem successful, and I know of no theory other than the respect-for-persons type that seems promising in this regard; thus, we should try to make some respect-for-persons theory work.

Even moving from this beginning, however, many options remain. I shall consider several possible interpretations of the respect-for-persons viewpoint, and I shall argue for one interpretation as best accounting for the relevant judgments. I then attempt to determine what answers to various questions about the uses of legal coercion best cohere with this interpretation and with other relevant judgments. The aim is to develop a coherent set of principles and judgments which yields plausible answers to questions we ask about the uses of law. Internal coherence is one of the most fundamental standards in the rational evaluation of thought in any sphere; a set of views which is internally coherent and also expresses widely shared considered judgments allows people to say what they want to say in a way that is not vulnerable to any well-established kind of rational criticism, for it is not clear that there are any standards of rational criticism which actually go beyond what is involved in the coherence standard. The method also offers some hope of reaching mutually satisfying and well-grounded conclusions on new and controversial issues.[3]

Most of what follows has to do with conditions which justify, or help to justify, the law's use of *coercion*. The concept of coercion may be usefully explicated by means of the idea of a "declared unilateral plan".[4] Someone attempting to secure the cooperation or compliance of another may have such a plan. The person's declared unilateral plan is what that person declares that he or she will do if the second person fails to cooperate or comply. Coercion is the attempt to secure compliance by means of a declared unilateral plan which is *prima facie* immoral, whether by the mere declaration of the plan or by its actual performance. Incarceration, the confiscation of money or other property, and threats to impose these are the most familiar aspects of law which make it coercive. In this study, the concern is with conditions which serve to justify the law's use of coercion.[5]

Having thus suggested that what follows is an attempt to build a framework within which questions about legal coercion may be answered, let me now provide an overview of that structure. This should help to place in context the discussions which follow. At the foundation of the structure is a fundamental principle expressing the basic commitment of respect-for-persons ethics. Chapter One explores questions concerning the initial interpretation of this commitment. Among other things, this principle denies the permissibility of interference with persons' control over their own lives, and it serves as the basic standard in terms of which more particular issues are to be evaluated.

Upon this foundation are to be placed subordinate principles which express the demands of respect-for-persons ethics with regard to more specific issues. In dealing with the ethics of legal coercion, these subordinate principles are of two major types. First, there are principles which indicate the purposes which can justify the use of legal coercion. These principles, which I call *inclusionary principles*, identify what may properly be included in the realm of legal coercion. Such aims as the prevention of conduct harmful to others, of conduct harmful to oneself, of offensive conduct, of immoral conduct, of human suffering and of damage to things other than persons, are to be considered here. If we can identify the aims which make the coercive intrusion of law legitimate, we can assess specific proposals for the use of law in light of those aims. Uses which do not serve a legitimate aim are to be rejected, while those which do have a valid purpose may be acceptable. Since the demands of respect-for-persons ethics are not always self-evident, much of what follows deals with the evaluation of possible inclusionary principles.

A second type of principle must also be considered, however. This is because the assessment of the legitimacy of particular uses of law is more complicated than can be allowed for through inclusionary principles alone. Some ways of pursuing even legitimate aims may be unacceptable, and because of this, additional principles must be recognized. These *exclusionary principles* indicate what must be excluded from the realm of legal coercion. If, for instance, an exclusionary principle of freedom of speech is recognized, it could be that some uses of law restrictive of speech would not be permitted even if aims authorized by inclusionary principles would be served. Thus, in evaluating legislation, one must not merely determine whether it is permitted by inclusionary principles, but also whether it is prohibited on special grounds such as are indicated in exclusionary principles. Since the two kinds of principles, taken together, express the demands of the respect-for-persons viewpoint, uses of law which comply with the principles are acceptable to that viewpoint. By working within this structure, we should be able to make well-grounded judgments about all kinds of uses of law.

Thus, in what follows I attempt to set out some main principles governing the proper use of legal coercion, doing so from the perspective of an ethics which assigns primary moral importance to persons. The aim is to contribute at once to both normative legal philosophy and to the theory of the ethics of respect for persons.

CHAPTER ONE

THE ETHICS OF RESPECT FOR PERSONS

1.1. INTRODUCTION

The ethical standard to be considered here finds its classical statement in the words of Immanuel Kant:

Act so that you treat humanity, whether in your own person or that of another, always as an end and never as a means only.[1]

Kant claims that human beings are to be treated in ways which respect the special moral status which persons have; they are to be treated *as persons*. Doing this can be understood to mean not using human beings as mere resources, respecting their autonomy, respecting their rights, respecting their choices. According to this principle, the test of whether an action is right is that of whether the action treats persons as persons or fails to do so. Those actions which fail to treat persons as persons are morally unacceptable. The principle is not restricted in its scope nor does it refer only to specific kinds of actions, and thus we have in this principle a standard with sufficient generality that it might be capable of serving as the single, fundamental moral principle in a system of moral thought.

Perhaps the most common complaint about this principle and the idea it expresses is that it is simply *too vague and too ambiguous* to serve adequately as a standard of right action. What, exactly, does it mean to treat someone *as an end* or *as a person*? All too often, the claim that some conduct fails to treat someone as an end or as a person seems to have nothing more behind it than the disapproval of the person making the claim. An adequate moral standard, however, would serve as a *basis* for such disapproval; unless the principle can be shown to have some reasonably determinate implications for the situations to which it is applied, it will fail to be fully satisfactory.

The present study makes use of a specific interpretation of the idea which lies behind this Kantian principle. I hope to show that the idea of treating persons as persons can be given an interpretation which not only yields determinate results for problematic cases, but also yields highly plausible results. My aim is not explication of Kant, but of an idea of which

1

Kant is the most famous exponent. My interpretation necessarily will differ in some respects from Kant's and those of other Kantians. Nonetheless, I hold that my interpretation is sufficiently close to what is important in Kant's to be considered Kantian. To explicate the interpretation used in this study, I shall identify some of the possible competing interpretations and draw some contrasts between those and the favored interpretation.

Kant himself makes some remarks which may provide some preliminary guidance. In discussing the application of his principle, Kant says that the person who violates it

intends to use another man merely as a means, without the latter containing the end in himself at the same time. For he whom I want to use for my own purposes ... cannot contain the end of this action in himself .... Instead, persons ... must always be esteemed ... only as beings who must be able to contain in themselves the end of the very same action.[2]

These remarks suggest that the crucial factor in determining whether or not a person is being treated as an end is whether that person could himself share the end or the goal involved. But this notion in turn depends upon what a person could *choose* as his or her end or purpose. In other words, treating someone as a person requires a certain *deference* to the person's own *choices*. This idea − that interaction with persons requires deference to their choices − is common to any minimally plausible understanding of treating persons as ends.

Difficulties surface, however, when we begin to investigate the claim that we must defer to the choices of persons. On one straightforward interpretation, the claim clearly seems to be false. No one thinks that we must always defer to the choices of others. One need not defer to an intruder's choice to shoot one's spouse; one need not defer to one's child's choice to consume the contents of the bottles in one's medicine cabinet. The idea that we must defer to the choices of others is thus far too restrictive to serve in a categorical way as a satisfactory moral standard. If the idea that deference is owed to the choices of persons is to be maintained, some qualification of that claim must be provided. The choices to which deference is owed must be distinguished from those for which that is not the case.

Competing interpretations of the idea of respect for persons may be understood as diverging at this point. That is, they provide different ways of qualifying the claim that persons' choices must be respected. Some dimension of a person or some subset of a person's choices may be identified as the appropriate object of respect. When the lines are drawn in different ways, the result is competing interpretations.

1.2. EMPIRICAL CHOICE

To help distinguish the options available here, let us refer to the actually expressed, empirically observable choices a person makes as the person's *empirical choices*. The straightforward interpretation of the idea of treating persons as persons mentioned above thus claims that each and every empirical choice must be respected. We have already seen that there is good reason to think that respecting persons as ends does not call for deference to every empirical choice. In addition, there are other reasons for rejecting this simple use of empirical choice.

One problem with empirical choice and empirical judgment generally is that it may vary over time. At one time a person may think that a certain action is the best thing to do, while later the same person may think the same action completely unacceptable; moreover, at the later time the person may think that the judgment or choice made initially was *wrong*. It is this latter possibility which presents serious difficulties for empirical choice as such, for in this kind of circumstance it is *impossible* to allow each empirical choice to determine events. Suppose that one Saturday afternoon Jones expresses his desire that he *never* be allowed to do some hazardous action; on Saturday night, however, Jones states that he wants to be allowed to perform the action. It is impossible to honor both choices. Thus, if treating persons as persons requires respect for each and every empirical choice, the second choice must be honored on Saturday night and the first choice honored only from the time it is expressed until a contrary choice is expressed. On this model, the will a person actually expresses at a given time is the will which must be respected.

Suppose, however, that on Sunday morning Jones returns to his earlier judgment that he should never be allowed to perform the hazardous action, and that he also expresses the judgment that he was wrong on Saturday night when he wanted to do it. Suppose also that Jones was intoxicated on Saturday night, but not at the other times. Further, at the other times, Jones was not in any state which could adversely affect his judgment. Respect for empirical choice as such requires that all three of these choices be given equal, indeed, absolute, weight at the time each is expressed. In this circumstance, does respect for persons really require that each choice be respected? To answer "yes" to this question would require that the intoxicated choice of Saturday night meet with no interference even if this meant that Jones would take action which would hinder the attainment of goals which it is known that he has, and which he expresses at other times. In a situation such as this, there is every reason to believe that the person (in some sense) does not want to do what he is actually doing. This forces a choice between greater weight being given to the person as a collection of distinct decisions or to the person as a continuous being. Since persons have continuity over time, the latter is a more plausible conception of a person. Thus, to respect a person is to respect a being continuous over time, and long-range goals seem a better guide to that sort of being than do isolated decisions.

Another aspect of this situation provides an additional argument against the simple use of empirical choice as the object of respect. The problem in the situation described is that of determining which choice to follow when an empirical choice at one time conflicts with an empirical choice at another time. In the above example, Jones himself, on Sunday morning, regards certain of his earlier choices as better than others; given an informed choice between his own judgment on Saturday afternoon and his judgment on Saturday night, Jones opts for the former. Thus, to give absolute weight to the choice actually expressed at any given time is to fail to give preference to a person's own best judgment.

Given these difficulties with taking simple empirical choices as the object of respect, we may next look to other more complex formulations.

1.3. RATIONAL CHOICE

The alternative to empirical choice which enjoys the most distinguished philosophical credentials is choice based on what we may call the *rational will*. The rational will is the will which would be expressed by any fully rational being and is a will which is determined in abstraction from the individual characteristics of such beings. This is a will which is free of the various inclinations, desires, and peculiarities of the many individuals who, although rational, are imperfectly so. The rational will is thus the expression of what is required or demanded by reason as such. This notion, of course, has played a role in the work of many philosophers, perhaps most notably in that of Kant, and has been given its most important recent manifestation in the work of John Rawls.

Use here of the notion of a rational will, however, admits of some variations. One possibility is to hold up the rational will itself as the sole object of respect. This would involve deference to the rational will and the rational will alone. Since only choices attributable to the rational will would then have moral significance, it would be possible to separate off a class of empirical choices — those not attributable to the rational will — which would not require respect.

The questionable feature of this possibility is the way in which it denies moral significance to all empirical choices. On this model, only rational choice deserves deference, and since rational choice is determined in abstraction from the individual characteristics of any person, an ethic based on this sort of choice would be very unrestrictive. The empirical choices of persons, and thus empirical persons as such, would drop out of consideration as a source of limitations on what others may legitimately do. On this model there would be no reason to give consideration to the expressed empirical objections of anyone, provided that a course of action sanctioned by rational choice is followed. Further, on this view there is no reason to avoid interference with *most* of the choices that people actually make. Most empirical choices depend on the contingencies of particular situations (what to have for dinner, where to go to college, whether to accept a job offer), and thus would be neutral from the point of view of the rational will, being neither demanded nor prohibited by that will.

Further, the idea of treating persons as persons is plausibly thought to require allowing persons to make *their own* choices and decisions and to require viewing those decisions as the responsibility of the person who makes them. Rational choice, however, is not plausibly regarded as a sort of choice which *belongs* to anyone in particular. Determined in abstraction from anyone's individual characteristics, rational choice can hardly be regarded as properly attributed to one person rather than another. No individual has the power to control the nature of the rational will and it is the same for all. By contrast, the demands of respect for persons make sense only if they are taken as demands concerning choices which can be said to belong to someone. Otherwise, one person's decisions would be *indistinguishable* from another's; only empirical decisions properly can be said to belong to individual persons. But the demands of respect for persons are demands about choices which *can* belong to and vary with individual persons. Thus, they are not demands about rational choice used in this way.

1.4. RATIONAL EMPIRICAL CHOICE

Perhaps more plausible would be the following use of the rational will. It could be argued that the proper object of respect in treating persons as persons is neither empirical choice as such nor rational choice as such, but is instead *the set of empirical choices which are not contrary to the rational will.* This possibility avoids the difficulty with the simple use of the rational will of not being identifiable as belonging to particular persons, since empirical choices are attributable to individuals. It also offers the prospect of avoiding the problem of empirical choice as such, since it does not require respect for each and every empirical choice, but only for those which do not violate the rational will. Further, it is plausible to think that this possibility is derivable from the idea of using rational choice alone, in that it could be argued that a perfectly rational being would choose to have its empirical choices respected, provided that they did not violate other expressions of the rational will.[3] Let us refer to this type of choice as *rational empirical choice.*

To determine whether a given choice is a rational empirical choice, it is necessary to reach some conclusion about what a rational person would do or choose in the relevant circumstances. A choice counts as a rational empirical choice if and only if it is not incompatible with the choice a rational person would make in the circumstances. The tenets of rationality are to be applied to the choice itself. Thus, if the question is that of whether the decision to undertake a certain course of action is rational, it must be determined whether a rational person would make that choice. The advantages and disadvantages of the alternatives would have to be weighed, and the best thing to do determined. If the empirical choice is incompatible with that, it does not require deference.

Whatever the attractiveness of the use of rational empirical choice as the object of respect, it does not yet seem to be what we need. One drawback of this approach can be seen if we consider some of the choices which would have to be respected under its terms. Take any fairly significant choice that a person might have to make where no single alternative is dictated by rationality alone. Choices about whether to quit a job, take a financial risk, get a divorce, commit an act of civil disobedience, risk or even take one's own life, or other weighty choices might serve as examples, for it is unlikely that any conception of rationality would dictate any particular decision for all such choices. If, for any such choice, risky or costly alternatives cannot be ruled out as necessarily irrational, then deference would have to be extended to the decision to pursue the risky or costly alternative *even if that choice is made in highly disadvantageous circumstances.* Suppose, for instance, that a couple decide to divorce during a heated argument. We may not find it objectionable to refuse to allow their decision to take effect immediately even if the decision to divorce cannot be shown to be irrational. But if rational empirical choice must be respected, choices such as these must be respected. That is to require deference unjustifiably to choices made under circumstances which render questionable even choices which are not irrational.

A further consideration may be seen in the following situation. Suppose that whenever Tom drinks too much, he finds that he has a strong desire to swim nude in a river that runs through the town in which he lives. Tom, we may suppose, has indulged this desire on some occasions in the past, and while he is a good swimmer so that his doing so is not particularly dangerous, he does have some concern that he may embarrass himself should the wrong people witness his activities. After giving the matter some thought, Tom asks the friends with whom he does his drinking not to allow him to go swimming when he is intoxicated; his friends agree. Now presumably there is nothing inherently irrational about swimming in the nude (or, if that seems wrong, substitute an example for which that is not the case), so that when, on the occasion of the next night on the town, Tom announces that he wants to swim nude, it is not possible to dismiss his decision as not being a rational empirical choice. We then face a dilemma similar to one faced in connection with simple empirical choice. We must choose between two conflicting expressions of will, both attributable to Tom and both satisfying the standards of rational empirical choice. If it is rational empirical choice that must be respected, then we must say that the intoxicated Tom who wants to swim nude has simply changed his mind and we must defer to his choice. If, on the other hand, we hold that we should respect Tom's earlier request that he not be allowed to swim nude rather than his intoxicated decision, then we fail to respect a rational empirical choice. Thus, by insisting that rational empirical choice must be respected, we impose an implausible restriction not only on how others may act in regard to persons making choices under disadvantageous circumstances, but also on how persons may restrict their own actions. Further, we deny the possibility of favoring what clearly seems to be a person's own best judgment in situations in which the person's empirical choices at different times conflict. Lastly, if persons are to be considered morally responsible for those choices to which deference is owed, then we deny the possibility of excusing persons from responsibility for rational empirical choices made under various difficult circumstances.

A defender of rational empirical choice might argue that these criticisms are unfair in that the substance of the idea of rational choice has not been considered. Perhaps if it were worked out, it would show that the sorts of empirical choices which have been taken to present problems for rational empirical choice as the object of respect are not rational after all. In that event, the foregoing criticisms would be undermined.

While it may not be possible to show that this *could not* be the result of a detailed theory of rational choice, it seems *very* unlikely that it would. Such a theory would have to show some rather extraordinary things. It would have to show that the rationality of various courses of action depend upon the procedures used to evaluate them. The same course of events could be rational or irrational depending on the state of the person deciding to pursue it. Suppose, for instance, Tom is considering going to graduate school. He considers the monetary cost involved, his own ability, his chances of getting a job afterward, the time it would take, how well he would like being in academic life, the expected financial return involved, and so on. He compares these with similar factors for the alternatives open to him, and on the basis of these considerations, some assessment of the rationality of Tom's going to graduate school may be reached. But surely the rationality of Tom's going to graduate school does not depend upon what state he happens to be in when he makes his decision; graduate school offers certain prospects for Tom which do not vary with temporary changes in his ability to weigh carefully the alternatives before him. Tom's graduate school prospects do not diminish simply because Tom gets drunk on Saturday night, only to revive the next day when Tom again is in full control. It is just that, however, which would have to be shown in order to deny that rational empirical choice is subject to the foregoing objections.

What must be remembered here is that rational empirical choice is not a matter of evaluating the rationality of making decisions while subject to the influence of such things as alcohol; rather, rational empirical choice is a matter of the rationality of pursuing various courses of action. It is a matter of the rationality of doing something in a specific circumstance, not a matter of the rationality of deciding about doing it while in a certain state. Thus, it might be suggested that these difficulties may be resolved by extending the notion of rational empirical choice to include consideration of the condition of the person choosing. That is, a choice might be deemed irrational not only because it is a choice to pursue an irrational course of action, but also because it is a choice made under conditions in which it is not rational to make choices (or, at least, not certain choices). In this way, deciding to do something not irrational in itself could be dismissed as not a rational empirical choice because of the circumstances in which it is made.

This suggestion pushes us in the direction of the interpretation favored in the present work, and its meritorious aspects are considered further below. What is not meritorious about this suggestion is the way in which it retains use of the idea that the rationality of a course of action may determine whether the choice to pursue it is to be respected. One problem with this — and with any use of rationality in this area — is that it depends upon a nonexistent theory of rationality. It simply does not seem to be the case that we have a sufficiently non-controversial conception of rationality to do the work asked of it here. It is hard to see how such a theory could be complete enough to do the job. However, even if we had such a theory, there is reason to think it should not be used to determine which empirical choices of persons are to be respected.

To put the point in one sentence, the objection to the idea that a decision to pursue an irrational course of action need not be respected is that persons may have a right to be irrational. Consider the case of another potential graduate student, Joe. Joe is a college senior and is considering going to graduate school because he wants to become a professor. However, Joe would be majoring in a crowded field in which competition for professorships is extremely intense; further, Joe is a rather mediocre student whose application for admission has been accepted only by a fourth-rate graduate program, no graduate of which has ever obtained employment as a professor. Even in this program there is every reason to think that Joe's performance will be unexceptional. To make matters even worse, the only reason why Joe wants to be a professor is that he hopes that as a professor be will have a great deal of leisure time; he imagines that he would have to work only ten or fifteen hours a week, and even that for only about two-thirds of each year. Now Joe considers his choice carefully; he is aware of his dismal prospects of ever obtaining employment as a professor, and he is also aware that every professor he knows seems to lead a quite harried existence. Nonetheless, Joe decides to go to graduate school.

Joe's decision to go to graduate school is irrational. Presumably, any adequate theory of rationality would include the principle that it is irrational to pursue an end by a means that is certain to fail; indeed, it has been held that the idea of rationality is exhausted by the choice of effective means. Joe's aim is to live a life of comparative leisure; his attempt to reach that goal by using graduate school in order to become a professor is certain to fail. But despite the irrationality of Joe's going to graduate school, does he not have the right to do it? Or, are we entitled to dismiss his carefully considered decision as not requiring our deference simply because it is

irrational? It is hard to see how a theory which purports to say that persons
are entitled to have their choices respected, could allow Joe's choice to be
so dismissed, yet that is what this use of rationality entails.

1.5. CONSIDERED CHOICE

What is next to be considered is the possibility that we avoid examining
the rationality of the courses of action between which a choice must be
made and instead focus on the procedures by which that choice is made
and on the condition of the person making the choice. In other words,
we may be able to identify those empirical choices which need not receive
deference *by the way in which they are made*. Choices reached by defective
means would then be the ones which need not be respected.

There are two major alternatives available along these lines. The proper
object of respect in treating persons as persons might be understood to
be only those empirical choices which actually satisfy certain *positive*
conditions, or it might be any empirical choice which is not marked by
the presence of certain *negative* conditions. The first alternative says that
deference must be extended to those choices made through reflection and
consideration of an ideal or nearly ideal sort. The choices to be respected
are those the person makes in the light of full information, in the absence
of pressure and with an appropriate amount of reflection and consideration;
arguments pro and con have been weighed and a settled view has been
reached. We may refer to choices of this sort as *considered choices*. The
first alternative thus says that treating persons as persons requires respecting
their considered choices.

The objection to this approach is that it fails to require respect for some
empirical choices which should be respected. Under the considered choice
approach, only choices made thoughtfully and deliberately qualify for
respect; yet surely many other choices persons commonly make, require
our deference. Relatively few choices that persons actually make meet
the standard imposed by the considered choice approach. Decisions about
what to have for dinner, what to do for an evening, whether to buy some
consumer product, what book to read, whether to attend a concert, and
so on, are often made in ways that could hardly qualify them as considered
choices, but surely they are definitely among the choices which require
others' deference. Further, there is no reason why many of these choices
should receive the sort of attention that would make them considered

choices. Carefully weighing decisions about such things as what to have for dessert, would often be absurd.

1.6. UNENCUMBERED CHOICE

The approach favored here is that which holds the proper object of respect to be those empirical choices of a person which lack certain negative features. Like the considered choice approach, this approach focuses on the conditions under which a choice is made rather than on the substantive merits of the choice, but this approach includes more empirical choices in the sphere to be respected since it is the absence of defects (so to speak) rather than the presence of virtues which qualifies a choice for that sphere. The defects which render a choice one to which deference is not necessarily owed shall be labeled *encumbrances*. Thus, respect is not required for a person's *encumbered choices*, and the proper object of respect in treating persons as persons is the *unencumbered will* of a person, that is, those of a person's empirical choices which are not encumbered.[4]

What is an encumbrance and when is a choice encumbered? An encumbrance is a feature of the circumstances in which a decision may be made or of the procedures through which a decision may be made. Let us refer to the circumstances of a decision and the procedures through which it is made as the *context* in which the decision is made. Sometimes decisions are made in contexts which hinder a person's ability to make the best decision, or, rather, some decision contexts embody features which hinder decision-making. We clearly recognize this phenomenon in many instances. A person chooses to go boating not knowing that a dangerous storm is approaching. Another agrees to an unreasonably expensive funeral within hours of learning of the death of a loved one and while under pressure from an unscrupulous funeral director. A third chooses to perform a dangerous stunt while intoxicated. Yet another chooses to make payments to a man because the man threatens to harm him if he does not. In these and similar cases we recognize that the choices made do not advance the aims of the persons making the choices, or at least that they may not advance the aims. Let us refer to decisions such as are found in these examples as *ineffective* choices. Encumbrances, then, are aspects of decision contexts which cause ineffective decisions. Decisions are encumbered only when they are made in contexts which embody some feature capable of causing ineffective decisions. The above decision to go boating is encumbered by the person's ignorance of the danger involved; the decision to have the overpriced funeral is encumbered by the emotional stress affecting that individual; the decision to perform the dangerous stunt is encumbered by the way in which the intoxicant affects the judgment of the person involved; and the decision to pay off the threatening man is encumbered by that man's threats. Hindrances to decision-making such as are found in these examples are what is meant by 'encumbrances'.

A particular decision is encumbered only if its context contains some feature which is capable of hindering the specific type of decision being made and that feature is likely to hinder the particular decision in question. These qualifications are required because, for one thing, some features of a decision context might be capable of hindering one kind of decision but not others. Ignorance of the time of day would be capable of causing errors in one's decisions about whether to leave now for an appointment but not (barring special circumstances) in one's decisions about whether to buy today's newspaper. The alleged encumbrance must also be likely to affect, or have affected, the decision in question, with unwanted results. Even if ignorance of the time of day is capable of causing a mistaken decision about whether to leave now, that decision is encumbered only if the time of day makes some difference in the correctness of the decision to leave. A decision is encumbered, then, only if some feature of the decision context is capable of hindering that kind of decision and is likely to hinder that particular decision. Encumbrances are features of decision contexts which are capable of hindering decision-making; particular decisions are encumbered when and only when they are likely to be, or have been, hindered by such a feature.

Encumbrances may be of various sorts. One distinction is that between general encumbrances and specific encumbrances. General encumbrances are those which interfere with decision-making across a range of situations or circumstances, while specific encumbrances are those which interfere only with some specific choice. Extreme retardation would presumably be a general encumbrance since it would hinder most of the retarded individual's choices. Ignorance of some specific fact about a specific situation would be a specific encumbrance, as for example in the case of someone climbing a ladder unaware of the fact that one of the rungs is cracked and cannot support a person's weight. Encumbrances may also be endogenous or exogenous. They are endogenous when the reason for the hindrance is something unusual about the person's ability to make choices, as in the case of someone so emotionally distraught that he cannot properly consider his alternatives. (The source of an endogenous encumbrance may of course be external; encumbrances are endogenous or exogenous depending upon the 'location' of the immediate hindrance.) An example of an exogenous encumbrance would be ignorance of some relevant fact about a course of action where the ignorance is due to some obstacle to obtaining knowledge of the fact. The ladder mentioned above may *appear* to be safe. The problem then is not a deficiency in the person's ability to make a choice, but is in the presence of an obstacle to attaining full information.

General kinds of encumbrances may cut across the classes of general/specific and endogenous/exogenous. Ignorance is clearly one major kind of encumbrance, and may take any of those forms. Other major kinds of encumbrance include such things as emotional stress, intoxication, many of the conditions labeled mental illnesses, and lack of consciousness. Compulsion would also count as an encumbrance in that it could prevent someone from giving effect to his or her choices. It is important to recognize, however, that what makes these things encumbrances is not that they prevent one's deliberations from living up to some theoretical standard of what it takes for choices to be proper or worthy of deference. Instead, encumbrances are identified as such by beginning with examples of cases which are generally recognized as involving choices which are not the sort that are the central concern of respect-for-persons ethics; those aspects of the decision contexts of such cases which cause the decisions to be suspect in this way are the encumbrances. Further cases can then be identified as encumbered or unencumbered by determining whether they involve such features as were discovered in these initial cases. Since the initial cases lead most clearly to such things as lack of information, lack of capacity to make use of information, and the presence of undue influence, these are the sorts of things most importantly looked for in further cases.

It is now possible to take a position on a central component of the idea of treating persons as persons. The choices which are of primary importance are the individual's *unencumbered* choices; respect for persons is, above all else, a matter of respecting these choices. This does not mean that encumbered choices require no deference, for a person may make an unencumbered choice that his or her encumbered choices be respected. The primary importance of unencumbered choices can be expressed in a statement which I shall refer to as the *principle of respect for persons*:

> All actions must be consistent with recognition of the supreme moral importance of each person's having control over his or her own life in accordance with his or her own unencumbered choices.

This principle is not self-explanatory. In this chapter I have endeavored to explain and defend my use of unencumbered choice as central to the idea of respect for persons. The greatest difficulty remaining is that of explicating the realm which composes a person's 'own' life. Most of the remainder of the present study is devoted to an attempt to define that realm with respect to its implications for the theory of the ethically acceptable uses of law, but even here questions will remain open. Nonetheless, it is important to have a statement of the basic ethical principle, for the views which follow are to be tested in part by reference to their plausibility as explications of the ethical commitment suggested by the principle of respect for persons.[5]

One final caveat: it should not be inferred from anything said here that the principle of respect for persons — as here stated — exhausts the sphere of morality. There may be additional moral considerations embodied in the idea of respect for persons, e.g., the importance of taking a certain view or attitude toward others.[6] However, the principle of respect for persons *does* exhaust the sphere of *enforceable* morality — the sphere of the more stringent moral requirements. Indeed, forcing a person to comply with some moral claim *violates* the principles respect for persons when the moral claim is not itself based on the principle of respect for persons. It is one of the tasks of what follows to render these remarks plausible.

CHAPTER TWO

THE NATURE OF A LIMITS THESIS

2.1. INTRODUCTION

With the following oft-quoted words, John Stuart Mill made the classical statement of what, in the present essay, will be called a *limits thesis*:

[T]he sole end for which mankind are warranted, individually or collectively, in interfering with the liberty of action of any of their number, is self-protection. . . . [T]he only purpose for which power can be rightfully exercised over any member of a civilised community, against his will, is to prevent harm to others. His own good, either physical or moral, is not a sufficient warrant . . . . The only part of the conduct of anyone, for which he is amenable to society, is that which concerns others. In the part which merely concerns himself, his independence is, of right absolute. over himself, over his own body and mind, the individual is sovereign.[1]

It is clear that Mill intends to claim that there are significant limits to the legitimate use of the law. This claim has been denied by others, among them Mill's best known contemporary critic Patrick Devlin,[2] who claims that there are no theoretical limits to the kinds of behavior which properly may be prohibited by law. The position presented in this study is, in part, a limits thesis, so it is of importance to be clear at the outset as to just what is being asserted by such a claim.

Devlin, of course, does take a position on the question of what uses of law are proper, e.g., when he claims that it is acceptable to use law to enforce conventional morality. Still, he and others have thought that there is some difference in kind between the views that he endorses and those of someone like Mill. Let us refer to the position of anyone who advances a view as to what uses of law are morally acceptable or unacceptable as a *theory of the proper uses of law*. Both Devlin and Mill hold theories of the proper uses of law. However, Mill claims that there are significant limits to the proper uses of law, while Devlin denies that theoretical limits are possible. We may then provisionally understand a limits thesis to be a theory of the proper uses of law which claims that there are theoretical limits to law comparable to those defended by Mill and attacked by Devlin. To move beyond this, we need to examine the issues which arise in connection with debate over and discussion of limits theses. Since the view advanced in this work is, like Mill's, a limits thesis, and since some have attacked limits theses as such, attention to these matters is desirable. Thus, in this chapter I attempt to clarify the kinds of claims that are being made by limits theses and to defend such theses against the general attacks that have been made on them. Readers interested only in the substantive positive claims defended in this work may wish to move directly to the next chapter.

2.2. DEFINING A PROTECTED SPHERE

Mill's limits thesis, as indicated in the above quotation, distinguishes two realms into which the conduct of any agent may be divided — that which "concerns others" and that which "merely concerns himself". The sphere of conduct which merely concerns an agent himself is for Mill the protected sphere into which the law must not trespass. Accordingly, the issue between advocates and critics of limits theses has often been taken to be that of whether it is possible to define a sphere of behavior which plausibly is to be left immune to interference from the law. Mill seems to be saying that there is such a protected sphere and offers a characterization of it. The critics of limits theses have been quick to attack Mill's description of the protected sphere and to deny that any plausible characterization of a protected sphere is likely to be forthcoming.

Numerous critics have attacked Mill on the grounds that all forms of human conduct affect or concern others, so that it is a mistake to attempt to isolate a sphere which does not.[3] For instance, Mill's nineteenth-century critic James Fitzjames Stephen writes:

I think that the attempt to distinguish between self-regarding acts and acts which regard others is like an attempt to distinguish between acts which happen in time and acts which happen in space. Every act happens at some time and in some space and in like manner every act that we do either does or may affect both ourselves and others. I think therefore that the distinction is altogether fallacious and unfounded.[4]

More recent critics adopt much the same viewpoint. Martin Golding asserts that "[w]e simply cannot isolate, once and for all, spheres of conduct which inherently are not harmful to others or of no concern to others", and claims that the central question is "whether the *kind* of conduct that is at issue is such that it is always self-regarding".[5] Ernest Nagel says that the issue is that of "whether there is a sharply delimited domain of human conduct that is by its very nature excluded from justifiable legal control",[6] and he casts doubt on the view that Mill's work "suffices to define categorically a realm of conduct that is inherently outside the scope of the law".[7] Similarly, Devlin argues that it is not "possible to drive a straight line across the field running from one end to the other, marking out for all time the private domain on one side and the public on the other".[8]

Criticisms of this sort can be given more than a single interpretation. These vary with different conceptions of what is being asserted in the claim that there is a protected sphere. Let us consider some of the possible interpretations.[9] One alternative is that a limits thesis simply asserts that there is a protected sphere, a realm of conduct in regard to which the law is not justified in interfering. Accordingly, suppose it is asserted that it is acceptable to use legal coercion only for a specified set of purposes. Whatever the purposes are, it will follow that it is not justifiable for the law to interfere in conduct which does not fall within the scope of the purposes. Acceptance of *any* limitation on the purposes *entails* that there is a sphere in which law may not legitimately interfere, viz, the sphere of conduct which lies beyond the scope of the purposes. Since even critics of limits theses accept some limits on the proper uses of law (a Devlin or a Stephen could perhaps agree, for instance, that law should not be used for the personal profit of public officials), this surely cannot be all there is to a limits thesis.

A second possibility is that the debate is over whether there are *action tokens* of the *action type* defined along the lines of the first possibility.[10] Accordingly, the critic may be saying that there are no token actions of the action type "actions beyond the scope of the proper purposes of legal coercion". Stephen, for instance, may have this claim in mind. However, there do seem to be actions beyond the scope of the purposes discussed in this context. Even if the approved purposes include enforcement of popular morality, there clearly remain action tokens not covered by the purpose (e.g., any action consistent with popular morality), and the same is likely to be true of any given set of purposes.

One proposal advanced to account for the issue here is that the essence of the debate is simply over the acceptable *purposes* for which coercive law may be used.[11] According to this view, the advocate of limiting law accepts only a restricted set of purposes for the use of coercive law and rejects the purposes advocated by others. Thus, someone like Mill claims that the only legitimate purpose for which coercive law may be used, is to prevent harm to others, and he rejects his critics' advocacy of purposes such as advancing a person's own good or preventing behavior popularly thought immoral. Further, on this interpretation of the debate the issue is not that of whether there is a protected sphere, so this approach does not reduce to triviality as do the ones just considered. There is, of course, a protected sphere defined by whatever purposes are deemed acceptable, but in viewing the debate as about the purposes themselves, we do not make the existence of a protected sphere the basic issue.

It is undeniable that the debate over the acceptable purposes for the use of coercive law is crucial to the matters here under study. However, the view that the debate is about what purposes are legitimate fails to capture the full complexity of this dispute. This can be seen if we consider the possibility that *agreement* as to the legitimate purposes might be obtained. The fact that all parties agree that legal coercion should be used only for a certain set of purposes is *not* sufficient to set *any* actual ethical limits to law. What constitutes *actual* limits to law? I shall assume that a thesis which allows all uses of law which governments are actually tempted to make would not be the sort of thesis which Mill and his followers intend, nor would it be the sort of thesis which would generate the kind of controversy which attaches to theses like that of Mill. There is something inherently *practical* about a limits thesis in that it says that law should not be used in ways that some actually want to use it. Further, this restriction applies even to the best of governments; a limits thesis not only provides an objection to uses of law undertaken by ill-intentioned, self-serving governments, but also limits what may properly be done by governments acting with the best of intentions. In other words, a limits thesis, to be worthy of the name, must have as a consequence that some uses of law advocated by, for instance, actual nineteenth- and twentieth-century legislators (even if they are presumed to be well-intentioned) in Great Britain and the United States, are ethically unacceptable. For this reason, it is not enough to have a limits thesis to assert merely that the law should be used only for certain limited purposes; in addition, a limits thesis must claim that some conduct that some are tempted to prohibit, falls outside the scope of the purposes.

This point is reinforced if we consider some of the disputes that have actually arisen over limiting law. It is possible to interpret some of Devlin's views as involving *acceptance* of the Millian claim that law should be used only for the prevention of harm to others. Devlin's attempts to show that behavior in violation of popular morality (e.g., homosexuality) can cause harm, are compatible with the claim that law should be used only to prevent harm.[12] Both Devlin and Mill might then be taken as agreeing on the question of what purposes law should be used to serve. But clearly this does not mean that there is no disagreement remaining between them; to understand their disagreement, one must look not only to the purposes for which law may be used, but also to what is said about the *application* of the principle that law should be used only for certain purposes.

A limits thesis involves claims about the purposes for which law may be used and also about how certain conduct stands with respect to those purposes. What is needed to complete this second aspect of a limits thesis is a factual understanding of various kinds of conduct. This understanding would enable the limits advocate to make and support claims that certain kinds of conduct are actually beyond the scope of the approved purposes, and disputes about whether certain kinds of conduct in fact cause harm (for instance), can be interpreted as disputes about that understanding.

The protected sphere defined by a limits thesis will be constituted by the kind of conduct which is found to lie, in fact, beyond the scope of the purposes for the use of legal coercion approved by the limits thesis. How is this kind of conduct to be described? If preventing harm is the approved purpose, then the kind of conduct beyond the scope of that purpose is conduct which causes no harm. This, of course, is the technique discussed above of defining the protected sphere in terms of the approved purposes. In the present context the trouble with this approach is that it leaves no room for the factual disagreements which arise in connection with limits theses; as was noted above, any restriction on the purposes for which law may be used must yield a protected sphere in this sense. What is required here is that the conduct which is protected be described in a way which is *neutral* with respect to the purposes in question.[13] In other words, we need descriptions of action types which are logically independent of the approved purposes. With such neutral descriptions of action types, we may then ask the question whether actions of each type do or do not fall within the scope of the purposes. Accordingly, we might understand a limits thesis as a thesis which claims that legal coercion should be used only for some limited set of purposes and that some neutrally described kinds of conduct in fact fall beyond the scope of those purposes.

The trouble with this latest interpretation of a limits thesis is that it seems to be one that allows limits theses to be refuted altogether too easily. Using harm prevention as the approved purpose, a limits thesis, on this interpretation, claims that some neutrally described kinds of conduct are harmless. Yet as the critics mentioned earlier have been quick to point out, it is far from clear that there is any kind of conduct which can never cause harm. For any action type, it seems likely that it may be possible to imagine circumstances in which a token action of that type is harmful:

Thus we can describe cases where such actions as throwing a stone into a pond or swimming the Channel *do* cause harm to others, e.g., in throwing the pebble into the pond we raised the water level sufficiently for the houses to flood; in swimming the Channel I caused the man who came to pick me up exhausted to drown. All that is needed to show that any action may cause harm to others is imagination.[14]

So on the present interpretation, a limits thesis appears easily defeated simply in virtue of the kind of claims it makes. Is the interpretation incorrect, is the appearance of easy refutation false, or is a limits thesis actually defeated on this point?

One intriguing proposal that would involve modifying the interpretation suggests that what should be claimed in a limits thesis is that an action type is properly subject to legal prohibition only if *all* tokens of that type fall within the scope of the approved purposes. If harm-prevention is the purpose, then this amounts to saying that prohibition of a kind of action is legitimate only if all token actions of that kind cause harm to others.[15] With this approach the claim that some imaginable circumstances can always be found in which some tokens of the action type in question cause harm, is rendered irrelevant; to make this limits thesis an empty assertion it would have to be shown that every action token causes harm. There is little doubt that such a limits thesis would divide off a protected sphere containing a wide range of action types.

The difficulty with this way of meeting the critics' charges is that it results in a thesis which sets more severe limits to law than even the limits advocate wants. For there are action types no one wants to exclude from prohibition, some tokens of which do not cause harm. These action types are thought to be properly subject to law because many or at least some tokens of the type do cause harm of a sort all parties to the debate agree should be prevented. Some apparent counter-examples of this type can be handled, however, so care must be taken to specify just what kinds of cases present the greatest difficulty for this approach. Risky actions such as driving dangerously or leaving attractive looking poisons where small children have easy access to them, appear to present problems for this approach, since not all tokens of these types result in harm. However, it is possible to regard the very fact of being put in jeopardy as a form of harm.[16] If we accept the idea that to be put at risk of harm is itself a form of harm, then all action tokens of risky action types do cause harm, namely, the harm of putting someone at risk of further harm. So the approach in question is not so easily defeated; however, it still cannot be accepted as adequate.

The kind of case that cannot be handled may be illustrated in the following example. Suppose it is proposed that the unauthorized use of explosive chemicals in populated areas be prohibited. Since the aim of this prohibition is the prevention of harm to those who might be within range of a chemical explosion, this is a prohibition the limits advocate is unlikely to oppose; but does the approach in question permit it? Not all instances of using explosive chemicals in populated areas result in harm to anyone, or even in explosions, so the occurence of harm through explosion is not enough to warrant prohibition. The creation of risk would be enough to justify prohibition when we consider cases involving negligent use of the chemicals. But what about the safe use of the chemicals by competent experts? The possibility that such persons might make unauthorized use of the chemicals means that not all tokens of the action type "using explosive chemicals in populated areas without authorization" put others in jeopardy; the expert's use of the chemicals does not create risk, and yet surely we may require even the expert to secure authorization so as to prevent incompetent or intentionally harmful uses. Another example might be the prohibition on driving while intoxicated. It is conceivable that some persons are capable of quite competent driving despite being intoxicated (especially where the level of alcohol in the blood serves as the criterion of intoxication), and if so, not all instances of driving while intoxicated place others in jeopardy. But since we have no way of reliably determining in advance who is competent to drive in this state, we consider ourselves justified in prohibiting all from such driving. We cannot prevent harm by prohibiting only incompetents from driving while intoxicated, since they are unlikely to judge themselves to be such. Thus, the only way to formulate the requisite legislation is to prohibit an action type – driving while intoxicated – not all tokens of which cause harm or even put others at risk. Thus, there is a general type of prohibition that seems reasonable but which cannot be accommodated on the approach in question. Action types tokens of which are often but not always risky cannot be prohibited on this approach when it is difficult to distinguish in advance whether a token is of the risky type. A limits thesis therefore should not be restricted in the way proposed.

If the above approach cannot be used in a limits thesis, such a thesis will have to define its protected sphere in a way that remains subject to the objection mentioned above. According to the above approach the protected sphere would be constituted by those neutrally described action types not all tokens of which fall within the scope of the approved purposes; the apparent alternative left by the unacceptable results of the use of that approach is that the protected sphere be constituted by those neutrally described action types *no* tokens of which fall within the scope of the approved purposes. Yet this way of defining the protected sphere is subject to the objection that there are no action types which satisfy the indicated conditions; for instance, it is subject to the objection that there are no action types no tokens of which ever cause harm. Again, the problem may be seen in a case such as the following.

Suppose it is proposed that tying one's left shoelace before one's right be prohibited. This would seem to be as clear a case as any of a prohibition that the limits advocate would oppose: surely, the limits advocate would insist, it is harmless to tie one's left lace first. Now comes the critic with a story designed to show that even this apparently innocent action type should not be beyond the reaches of the law: some diabolical person has rigged things in such a way that if Jones ties his left lace first, it will trigger an explosion killing many innocent persons; even left-first shoelace tying *can* cause harm to others. So that action type is properly subject to legal prohibition.

There is, however, a way out for the limits theorist. A limits thesis can be construed as making still another kind of claim that is not even susceptible to the present objection. We must consider again exactly what a limits thesis must say about the action types which compose the protected sphere. I shall argue that a limits thesis need not even claim that action types in the protected sphere have no tokens which fall within the scope of the approved purposes. To advocate the harm principle one need not claim that there are any action types incapable of causing harm; limits theorists may have made such claims, but they *need not* have done so. What is crucial to the basic aim of a limits thesis is not that the protected actions be necessarily harmless, but that *the prohibition of an action in fact serve the approved purposes for the use of legal coercion*. Something like the harm principle is respected when and only when there is a connection between the prohibition of some specific kind of behavior and the reduction of some specific kind of harm; with such a connection prohibition serves the purpose of preventing harm; without it, it does not.

The kind of counter-example we have been concerned with can now be met. It may be conceivable that left-first shoelace tying might cause harm, but the world as we know it is so constituted that the prohibition of left-first shoelace tying would not serve to reduce any specific kind of harm. There might be freak occurrences of harm that would be avoided if such a prohibition were enacted, but such unforeseeable effects do not permit us to say that the prevention of harm will be served by the prohibition. Other examples of this type can be met in the same way. The critic of limiting law claims that no kind of action can be placed beyond the reach of law because of that one-in-a-million chance that a token of any action type may cause harm; the objection misses because that kind of connection between the action type and harm is not sufficient to warrant the claim that prohibition of actions of that type will serve to prevent harm. The point that the limits advocate should emphasize is not that behavior composing the protected sphere cannot be harmful, but that prohibition of behavior in the protected sphere will serve no legitimate purpose.

On my view, then, the vital claim that a limits thesis must make about neutrally described kinds of conduct is that their prohibition will serve no approved purpose; the protected sphere will be composed of those kinds of conduct prohibition of which would be pointless in this sense. It remains highly relevant, of course, to claim that certain kinds of conduct are harmless, but this is because the prohibition of harmless conduct is likely to be pointless, not because harmlessness itself is crucial. Unless we have good evidence of causal connections such that prohibition of a kind of conduct will serve approved purposes, a limits thesis claims that we have no right to impose the prohibition.

One further point is needed to mark off the differences between a limits advocate and a critic such as Devlin. Devlin himself is willing to say that "[n]othing should be punished by the law that does not lie beyond the limits of tolerance".[17] He thus allows that at a given time prohibition of some kinds of conduct may not in fact serve the approved purposes. The difference between the limits advocate and Devlin on this point is that the limits advocate does not allow that a type of conduct can *come* to satisfy the valid purposes of legal coercion merely because *people's attitudes* toward the conduct change. So Devlin and the limits advocate might agree that in, say, the U.S.A. in 1980 premarital sex should not be prohibited. Devlin, however, would claim that premarital sex would properly be prohibited if people came to view that conduct (as perhaps they once did) with "intolerance, indignation, and disgust". This the limits advocate must deny. But this does not mean that other kinds of new information could not change the status of a type of conduct under a limits thesis. If it were discovered that premarital sex causes some great harm, that could very well change the evaluation of prohibition of such conduct. Thus, a limits thesis claims not only that there are some neutrally described kinds of conduct prohibition of which will not serve the approved purposes, but also that changes in attitudes toward the conduct would not be sufficient to bring the conduct within the scope of approved purposes.

The criticisms of limits theses mentioned at the beginning of this section thus do not succeed, for they misconstrue, in one way or another, the nature of the claims which must be made in a limits thesis. The objection just discussed falsely supposes that a limits thesis must claim that some kinds of conduct are necessarily harmless. Other aspects of the critics' charges may now be seen to depend upon similar assumptions. One worry is whether we can define a protected sphere valid 'once and for all' or 'for all time'. In one sense a limits thesis clearly can and must do this: a limits thesis claims that conduct prohibition of which will not serve the purposes it approves should be in the protected sphere 'for all time'. But this does not entail that a limits thesis must say that there is any particular kind of *neutrally described* behavior which must be placed in the protected sphere for all time, if that means it must be so placed even if new facts come to light. A limits thesis need only claim that some neutrally described kinds of behavior should be placed in the protected sphere given present information about them. It is perfectly consistent with a limits thesis to allow that various kinds of conduct should be considered on a case-by-case basis and that our view of conduct previously considered might have to be revised in the light of new information about it and the benefits of its prohibition.

Another worry raised by critics of limits theses concerns the way in which such theses characterize the protected sphere. It sometimes seems to be assumed that a limits thesis must provide a single, neutral description of that sphere. Of course it is extremely unlikely that there is any single, neutral action type all tokens of which fall in the protected sphere, so if one thinks a limits thesis must provide this, one is likely to think limits theses implausible. Of course, a limits thesis need not provide such a characterization of the protected sphere. What it should provide as a single, comprehensive, characterization is the non-neutral description of the protected sphere in terms of the approved purposes. What it should provide by way of neutrally described action types is simply the various specific action types prohibition of which will not serve the purposes.

If what a limits thesis must say about a protected sphere 'not the law's business' can thus be saved from objections that such claims are misguided in their very form, what must a limits thesis say about the legitimate aims of legal coercion? Limits advocates have typically opposed the enforcement of morality while endorsing the use of law to prevent harm. Let us consider what this says about the nature of a limits thesis.

2.3. ENFORCING MORALITY VERSUS PREVENTING HARM

Advocacy of the enforcement of morality is sometimes placed in sharp contrast to advocacy of the enforcement of prohibition on harming others. For example, Joel Feinberg seems to be relying on this contrast when he compares the use of law to prevent harm to others with the state's "enforcing a truly rational morality as such",[18] and David A. Conway attributes such a view to H. L. A. Hart: "[t]he position that Hart sets out to defend is that society has no right to prohibit any action simply on the ground that it is immoral; the only actions with which society may interfere are those which are likely to cause harm".[19] Similarly, the view is attributed to Mill by Bayles: "Mill and his defenders deny that the immorality of conduct, in and of itself, is ever a good reason for legislation limiting liberty".[20] The view is that while it is acceptable for the law to be used to force people not to harm others, it is not acceptable for the law to be used to force people to behave morally. The coherence of this view becomes questionable, however, when one inquires into what is involved in forcing people not to harm others. For one thing, harming another certainly seems to be an instance of behaving immorally, at least in the absence of some special justification. Further, it seems reasonable to suppose that the reason why it is acceptable to use the law to prevent people from harming others is just because harming others is morally wrong. What other reason could there be to justfiy the prohibition on harming others?[21] Even if, after a utilitarian fashion, one cites the undesirable effects the permitting of harming others would have on the general welfare as the justification of the prohibition, one has in that very claim a reason for charging the act of harming another with immorality. Still, it might be suggested that a utilitarian approach is not committed to the view that the reason why the prohibitions it permits are acceptable is because the prohibited behavior is immoral. The utilitarian may instead be claiming that the reason why the prohibition is acceptable is because of the desirable effects of the general prohibition, rather than because of the undesirable effects of the individual actions prohibited. For example, an individual action of walking across the grass might have no undesirable effects and yet it could still be advantageous to prohibit all such acts for the sake of avoiding the undesirable effects that would derive from many instances of walking across the grass. This could be taken to be a case of justifying a prohibition on grounds other than that the actions prohibited are morally wrong.

This approach fails to save the contrast between preventing harm and preventing immorality, however. One reason why it fails is that it shows (at best) only that the immorality of an action is not a necessary condition for its prohibition. The immorality of an action still constitutes a strong reason in favor of its prohibition even in terms of the utilitarian approach in question, since the conditions which count in favor of regarding an action as immoral (e.g., causing unnecessary unhappiness) also count in favor of prohibition of the action. The fact that the immorality of the action may not be sufficient to justify its prohibition does not save the contrast either, since advocates of the enforcement of morality are not committed to the view that all immoralities must be prohibited.

There is a deeper reason for suspecting this contrast between preventing harm and preventing immorality as well. The very nature of the question faced by a theory about the proper uses of law commits the theory to the view that it is acceptable to enforce the requirements of morality. The question faced by this sort of theory is, roughly, that of when it is ethically permissible to prohibit conduct through law; an answer to this question will assert that the prohibition of conduct through law is ethically permissible when certain conditions are met. Different theories will impose different conditions in answer to the question, but whatever conditions are advocated, the theory will be one which asserts that legal prohibition of conduct is defensible when and only when sound ethics permits or requires it. Suppose, for instance, that one adopts a utilitarian approach and asserts that adherence to the demands of the principle of utility requires that only conduct which is harmful to others, and not conduct which is harmful only to agents themselves, be prohibited. This is to say that legal prohibitions are to be imposed only when morality (in this example, utilitarianism) says so. Any theory which purports to resolve the issue before us will be a theory which advocates the enforcement of morality in at least some sense. So, however useful the contrast between enforcing morality and preventing harm may be for some purposes, it does not suffice to define the essential issues in the debate between advocates and opponents of limits theses.

2.4. POSITIVE MORALITY VERSUS CRITICAL MORALITY

One way to make sense of the contrast between preventing harm and preventing immorality is to distinguish positive morality from critical or discriminatory morality.[22] Positive morality, that is, the morality commonly accepted in a society, does not necessarily coincide with critical or discriminatory morality, which is defined as a moral viewpoint that meets more demanding standards than merely being generally accepted by the people in a society. The exact nature of these standards varies from theory to theory, but the basic idea common to all is that critical morality is rationally defensible in ways that positive morality sometimes is not. With this distinction, it is possible to assert a limits thesis which says that critical morality permits the enforcement of harm prevention, but prohibits the enforcement of positive morality *qua* positive morality.

This interpretation does contribute to understanding the nature of a limits thesis. Such a thesis is a claim about the demands of a morality which is held to meet the standards of critical morality, and the influential versions of limits theses do claim that positive morality is not to be enforced for its own sake. However, it is not sufficient to understand the debate as merely a matter of whether critical morality permits the enforcement of positive morality, for, as we shall see in the following sections, this ignores important issues which can be seen in certain other interpretations of the nature of this issue. So, while important, the contrast between positive and critical morality does not take us far enough.

2.5. WHICH CRITICAL MORALITY SHOULD BE ENFORCED?

The distinction between different forms of morality allows for an interpretation of the debate according to which it is about what morality to enforce. Limits theorists claim that only a certain morality should be enforced and that other moralities should not be, while their opponents advocate enforcement of competing moralities. Here different theorists rely on different critical moralities in setting forth different theories about the morally proper uses of law. It is thus possible to interpret the debate over limits theses as a debate over the question of which critical morality should be enforced.[23]

Suppose we take a utilitarian morality as an example again. The utilitarian, let us say, advocates a limits thesis similar to Mill's. In doing so, the utilitarian may differ with others over such questions as that of whether homosexual conduct should be prohibited. Someone advocating a morality based on the Bible, for instance, might take the opposite view on the homosexual issue. But what is the source of the differences between the utilitarian and the Biblical moralist? According to the interpretation now in question, the real issue is that of which morality should be enforced The utilitarian advocates the enforcement of *utilitarian* morality, while the Biblical moralist advocates the enforcement of *Biblical* morality. On this view, the debate is wholly a theoretical one about what is the most defensible morality. This interpretation is bolstered by recognition of the fact that limits advocates have typically been utilitarians who have not only advocated limiting law, but also have put forth utilitarian morality as an ethical system superior to others. Further, the above considerations regarding the contrast between preventing harm and preventing immorality also lend support to this interpretation, since it was argued there that preventing harm is an instance of preventing immorality and since the justification of enforcing harm prevention would thus require the working out of a critical morality which would compete with other proposed moralities.

However, this interpretation of the debate is also guilty of over-simplification. That a limits thesis is not merely a thesis about which morality should be enforced, can be seen if one considers the possibility of a case in which there is agreement as to the nature of the most defensible morality but disagreement as to whether particular kinds of conduct should be prohibited. For instance, two persons who agree that utilitarianism is the most defensible morality need not both be limits theorists. The utilitarian who is a limits theorist argues that certain conduct contrary to popular morality (homosexuality may again serve as an example) causes no harm to anyone, while its prohibition does cause harm, so that, on balance, prohibition is undesirable. The utilitarian who opposes limits theses, however, argues that conduct contrary to popular morality is harmful in that it weakens the bonds that hold society together, so that its prohibition should not be disallowed. Here there is agreement as to the correct morality, but disagreement on the question of limiting law. A limits thesis cannot be wholly a thesis about which morality should be enforced.[24]

2.6. WHICH SPECIFIC KINDS OF CONDUCT ARE IMMORAL?

When the debate over limiting law is put in terms of our last example, that is, in terms of a debate between two persons who agree on the nature of morality but disagree over whether particular forms of conduct should be prohibited, another way of interpreting the debate suggests itself. The debate might be understood as one over the morality of the conduct whose prohibition is in question. This interpretation is like the last in that it makes the debate a matter of assessing the morality of conduct, but differs from it in that on the previous interpretation differing assessments of conduct were due to the use of different moralities, while on the present interpretation differing assessments of conduct are due to different perceptions of the character of the conduct itself, rather than of the morality used to evaluate it.[25]

One example which supports this interpretation is the one just mentioned, that in which there is disagreement over whether conduct contrary to popular morality causes harm. Other examples conform to this interpretation as well. One reason why one might oppose the prohibition of such things as homosexuality, pornography, prostitution, and so on, is the belief that there is nothing morally wrong with those things. Such claims may be based on the view that the behavior in question lacks any characteristic which warrants regarding it as contrary to the standards of an agreed-upon morality, and in such cases the debate over its prohibition fits this interpretation.

Once again, however, the nature of the debate is over-simplified by this way of viewing it. The possibility of debate over the nature of the morality to be used in assessing particular kinds of conduct means that this interpretation also does not capture the full complexity of the issues with which we are here involved. Even when there is agreement as to the character of the actions being assessed, this does not guarantee that the differences between the advocate and the opponent of a limits thesis will not be present, for those differences may be due to the use of differing moral viewpoints. Differences in assessment of the character of specific kinds of conduct may account for some of the disputes which arise in this area, but not all of them.

2.7. PROCEDURAL MATTERS AND DEMOCRACY

The debate over the limits of law has also been construed in another way, rather different from any of those considered above. The controversy can be seen as a matter of the *procedures* used in deciding what legislation to enact. Both those who oppose limiting law and their critics sometimes see the question in this way. One approach is to claim that commitment to democracy means that the enforcement of popular morality cannot be ruled out.[26] To deny the acceptability of the enforcement of popular opinion would appear to be tantamount to denying that 'the people' should make the final decisions with respect to their own governance, since any procedure which could guarantee that final decisions not be determined by merely popular opinion would have to remove the final decision from the hands of the public. Hence, opposition to the enforcement of popular morality can be made to appear elitist and anti-democratic.

Certain responses to other claims made in defense of the enforcement of positive morality also tend to support the view that the debate primarily concerns the question of the procedures to be used in deciding what legislation to enact. The appeal to positive morality means that some prohibitions will be based on commonly held feelings of "intolerance, indignation, and disgust" at the activities prohibited.[27] This position may be attacked on the grounds that it fails to require that sufficient care be taken in deciding to prohibit; it fails even to ask that the feelings leadings to prohibition be more than mere prejudices or that any sort of rational assessment of the feelings be made.[28] The critic of the enforcement of positive morality thus sometimes bases his case on the demand that certain restrictive procedures be used in legislative decision-making, and the debate over the limits of law can be seen as a debate about these procedures. The opponent of limiting law claims that democratic procedures preclude limits, while his critics claim that sound procedure precludes the enforcement of mere positive morality.

However important these procedural issues are for some purposes, their primary contribution to the question of the limits of law is one of mere confusion. These procedural issues are raised in connection with the question of how a society ought to go about reaching a collective decision regarding the uses of law. Democratic procedures are typically advocated here and those participating in the democratic processes are at least encouraged to weigh calmly and rationally the issues on which they are voting. The procedure for reaching group decisions is to be one of placing authority in the hands of the majority of (hopefully) well-informed and rational voters. But how should each voter vote? That is, what methods should a responsible voter use to evaluate proposed legislation? It is (to say the least) no help at all to say that each voter should be guided by the will of the majority, since the answer to our question is to determine the will of all responsible voters. This indicates that the problem faced by someone in a position to contribute to the enactment of legislation (e.g., a voter or a legislator) is importantly different from the problem of how a group should reach collective decisions. The voter-legislator needs criteria for the evaluation of legislation which he or she may use prior to and independently of knowledge of the votes of others on the same legislation. From the perspective of the voter-legislator, all of these worries about the procedures that a group should use in reaching its decisions are fundamentally irrelevant. The voter-legislator is concerned not with questions of how group decisions should be reached, but with the question of what legislation is worthy of support. (Knowing this, the voter-legislator can then attempt to have the legislation enacted by the society through whatever group decision procedures are used by the society.) In other words, the voter-legislator is concerned with what the *substance* of the law ought to be, not with what *procedures* a group should use in forming the law.

Once this distinction is made, it is clear that a limits thesis is aimed at the problem faced by the voter-legislator, not with the problem of the best group-decision procedure. A limits thesis claims that certain kinds of legislation ought not to be enacted, and that is just the kind of claim a responsible voter-legislator will be concerned with, and is a claim that is compatible with a variety of group-decision procedures (an absolute monarch could follow the dictates of a limits thesis). Thus, however important democracy is, however important it is that those voting in a democracy be encouraged to use rational methods in deciding how to vote, all of that is irrelevant to the question of the validity of any limits thesis. Commitment to democracy as a group-decision procedure says nothing about what kinds of legislation ought to be supported by those participating in democracy. Thus, to understand the debate over limits theses as a debate about the procedures to be used in reaching group-decisions, is to misunderstand the debate.

Failure to distinguish the group-decision problem from the voter-legislator problem often leads to difficulties. Bayles, for instance, argues that we should not advocate the enforcement of anyone's critical morality, for such a morality might differ so much from the popular morality, that instability would result.[29] This seems to me to misconstrue the issue. A limits thesis purports to tell us what kinds of legislation are defensible and in doing so it appeals to a critical morality (see 2.3 above). However, such a thesis could lead to instability only if it were used to impose legislation on a group, that is, if it were used as a group-decision procedure. If not used as a group-decision procedure, an advocate of a limits thesis would have to work through the group-decision procedure in use to see that the limits were respected. If the group-decision procedure is reasonably democratic, then either the demands of the limits thesis will be fairly close to those of the popular morality or the limits thesis will be violated. In neither case does the appeal to a critical morality as the best guide to legislation lead to instability.[30]

2.8. CONCLUSIONS

A limits thesis is a thesis which expresses moral judgments about the proper uses of legal coercion. As such it involves an appeal to some general principle or principles of morality. The principle(s) of morality are applied to certain relatively specific moral issues; in particular, the principle(s) of morality are applied to the question of what purposes legal coercion properly may be used to serve. A limits thesis thus expresses judgments about the accept-able aims of legal coercion. These judgments clearly may have as a conse-quence the claim that it is not justifiable to use the law to enforce popular morality as well as for various other purposes. Perhaps less obvious is the fact that these judgments need not be equivalent to the assertion that any critical morality should be enforced. For while it is true that a limits thesis necessarily approves the enforcement of the claims of some morality in what it says about the proper uses of law, a limits thesis need not approve pro-hibition even of all forms of conduct deemed immoral by the very morality on which the limits thesis is based. A limits thesis may be based upon a morality which supports the view that only some kinds of immoral conduct are properly subject to coercion; when it is so based, some claims about which kinds of immorality are properly subject to coercion will be part of the limits thesis. Thus, while a limits thesis does support the enforcement of some moral judgments, it need not and typically will not support the view that even genuine immorality as measured by its own moral presuppositions is a good reason for legal prohibition. Instead, such a thesis will claim that only certain important kinds of immorality warrant prohibition. These prohibitable immoralities may be described as violations of persons' *rights*. As I shall use the expression " ... has a right to ... ", to say that a person has a right to something is to say that others are subject to an enforceable moral requirement (duty or obligation) to accord that thing to that person.[31] A limits thesis asserts that there are some moral requirements which involve rights so as to be enforceable, but that there are other moral claims (valid or invalid) which are not properly enforceable, and whose enforcement would itself violate rights.

In addition to expressing moral judgments about the proper uses of legal coercion, a limits thesis also makes further claims about the application of those judgments to particular kinds of behavior. Its claim is that there are some kinds of conduct which fall beyond the scope of the approved purposes for the use of legal coercion and whose status as being in this protected sphere cannot be changed by mere changes in public opinion. These kinds of conduct are to be described in a way that is neutral with respect to the purposes approved by the limits thesis and they are to be beyond the scope of the purposes in the sense that, given available infor-mation, it is not the case that the prohibition of these kinds of conduct will serve the purposes. The protected sphere defined by a limits thesis is thus composed of those kinds of conduct which do not fall within the scope of the purposes in this sense.

This said, it is now possible to respond to one further criticism of limits theses. It has been charged by at least two writers that limits advocates are guilty of a kind of circularity in the way they use moral judgments to determine what kinds of conduct may be interfered with. Golding asserts against Mill that "it does no good to say that . . . conduct is taken out of the 'self-regarding' class in case of [violations of specific duties and obligations to others], unless we have already determined what the duties and obligations are. But this is precisely what Mill's principle, with its distinction between self-regarding and other-regarding conduct, is supposed to help us determine".[32] Similarly, Alan Wertheimer claims "that the harm principle does not seem capable of resolving [questions about what constitutes harm], at least without appeal to certain moral judgments about the kinds of things people should be required to do. But it is those moral judgments which the harm principle is meant to support, and to use those judgments in defining harm to others would clearly be putting the cart before the horse".[33]

These criticisms misconstrue the relationships involved. A limits thesis applies general moral considerations to the problem of defining such concepts as harm, and then in turn uses the results of that application to support judgments about the status of particular kinds of conduct. There is no circularity, but instead an increasingly specific application of general moral principles. So the judgments the harm principle is meant to support are judgments about whether specific kinds of conduct should be subject to legal prohibition. Since what is needed to define harm is a general understanding of the kinds of things people should be required to do, the objection misses its mark.

With this understanding of the nature of a limits thesis, we can now see how a variety of different kinds of disputes may arise concerning such theses. Disputes may arise concerning the nature of the critical morality presupposed by a limits thesis, over the set of purposes for the use of legal coercion approved by the critical morality in question, or over whether various specific kinds of conduct do or do not fall within the scope of the purposes. To have a limits thesis, one must advance a critical morality which restricts the purposes for which legal coercion may be used in such a way that the prohibition of some kinds of conduct does not serve the purposes. Let us turn next to the substance of such a thesis.

CHAPTER THREE

THE HARM PRINCIPLE

3.1. HARM AND INTERESTS

The moral foundation of the thesis advanced here is the principle which requires that persons be treated as persons, and that requires that each person's unencumbered choices be respected, at least within a certain sphere. A vital element in the theory of the ethical limits of law is the determination of what that sphere is. Within that sphere, a person's own unencumbered choices must be allowed to have effect in action, and others' choices, whether or not expressed through law, must not interfere. This notion serves both to provide one of the main justifications for the use of legal coercion, and to provide the basis for the limitation of law.

A justification for the use of legal coercion is provided in this way. The actions of individuals as well as those of governments may interfere with a person's choices, and when they do they are in violation of the principle of respect for persons. Prevention of such actions provides one of the legitimate aims of legal coercion. Law may be used to interfere with actions of this kind. The principle which asserts that a good reason for the use of legal coercion is provided by such aims is known as *the harm principle*.

As its name implies, the notion of *harm* is central to what is asserted in the harm principle. Legal coercion may be used to prevent people from *harming* others. Much therefore depends upon the question of what constitutes harm. Understood broadly enough, the concept of harm could include virtually everything that even opponents of limits theses would like to see prohibited; thus an effective limits thesis must provide a conception of harm restrictive enough to exclude some of the controversial uses of law. Typically, harming someone is understood as violating the person's interests.[1]

If harm is the invasion of interests, then everything turns on the question of what a person's interests are. Unfortunately, this move seems to raise more questions than it answers, for what are a person's interests? Interests might be understood in terms of whatever a person (empirically) wants. However, this approach does not seem to be satisfactory when used in conjunction with the harm principle, for it is not always unacceptable to deny persons what they want. Further, persons sometimes want things which are not in their interests and do not want things which are in their interests. Tom, for example, wants to inject the contents of a certain syringe into his veins, not knowing that it will kill him if he does so; conversely, Mary does not want to receive an injection (with a syringe containing a different substance!), falsely believing that it will not cure her disease.

Alternatively, interests may be understood in a more objective way. A person has an interest in something if it is objectively *of value* to the person,[2] if it is objectively *good* for the person,[3] or if she "stands to gain or lose depending on [its] condition or outcome".[4] One may thus have an interest in something one does not want.

Unfortunately, this approach seems to demand a theory of what is objectively good for a person, of value to her, and so on. Without such a theory, we have no way of resolving controversial cases. Is it, for instance, in a person's interests to be allowed to view pornographic movies? Without a theory of objective good, we lack a means of resolving the differences of opinion likely to manifest themselves when different individuals answer that question. The problems of developing such a theory seem likely to be even more cumbersome than the problems which led to the need for it.

In addition, a theory of interests which defines interests in terms of what is objectively valuable or good for a person, seems too broad for use in conjunction with the harm principle. For surely it is not reasonable to allow the use of coercion to prevent all actions which interfere with someone's interests so understood. This would mean that a person's actions could be restrained whenever they worked to the disadvantage of others, regardless of the question of who is entitled to the benefit. Mary's getting a certain job rather than Bob works to Bob's disadvantage, and is not in his interest, but Bob is not thereby *harmed* in a way which brings this act of hiring within the scope of the harm principle.

This objection might be avoided by restricting the class of harms to which the harm principle applies. Stipulating that the term 'injury' be used for the harms to which the harm principle applies,[5] Michael Bayles also adopts the interest interpretation of harm. For Bayles, interests are to be understood in terms of the complete set of a person's wants: "Thus, 'L is in X's interest' is equivalent to 'L would make X more able to fulfill his self-regarding wants (everything considered)' ".[6] To injure someone is to damage his or her interests or to create an unreasonable risk of such damage.[7] The notion of injury is further qualified by a version of the *Volenti* maxim: "a person is not injured by actions contrary to his interest if he voluntarily

participates in the activity of which they are a part".[8] Bayles also wants
to distinguish injury from non-benefit, and does so by defining injury as
action which makes another person *less able* to fulfill his or her wants,
and non-benefit as action which fails to make another person *more able* to
fulfill wants.[9] This may provide a response to the claim that Bob (mentioned
in the preceding paragraph) is not harmed by the act of hiring not in his
interest, since the act of hiring someone else may be interpreted as merely
a failure to promote Bob's interests.

However, there remains an objection to be made to this analysis of injury.
For it is not clear that every act of making a person less able to fulfill his
wants belongs under the harm principle. Suppose that Bill very much wants
to purchase a piece of land which is for sale, but that before Bill is able to
raise the necessary money, the land is purchased by Linda. Linda's purchase
of the land makes Bill less able to satisfy his wants, and thus is contrary to his
interests ('injures' him). Linda's action is not merely a failure to benefit Bill,
for we would not say that Linda had benefited Bill had she not purchased the
land, knowing nothing of Bill's interests in it. Thus, although Linda's action
is contrary to Bill's interests, that fact alone does not seem to provide even
a presumption against it.

Another approach involves understanding harm as the "impairment of
a being's welfare interests".[10] Welfare interests, in turn, may be understood
as "those interests which are indispensable to the pursuit and fulfillment of
characteristically human interests, whatever those interests might be".[11]
This approach, it seems to me, accords fairly well with general use of the
concept of harm, but does less well as an explication of the concept of harm
as used in the harm principle. Used in the harm principle, the concept of
harm is supposed to identify ways of affecting others which are properly
subject to interference, particularly by the law. To understand harm as the
impairment of welfare interests would seem to unduly restrict the scope of
justifiable legal intervention. Stealing ten dollars from a man who would
not even notice the loss would not impair his welfare interests, yet it is
uncontroversial that such actions fall under the harm principle.

Now I do not assume that these remarks about harm and interests con-
clusively undermine the attempt to understand harm in terms of interests.
However, I think the difficulties with that attempt do suggest that it may
be worthwhile to look elsewhere for understanding of the notion of harm,
especially as that notion is used in the harm principle. The plan of the present
study demands that we look to the principle of respect for persons.

3.2. A RESPECT-FOR-PERSONS CONCEPTION OF HARM

A respect-for-persons understanding of the concept of harm will define harm in terms of the taking from others of choices which are rightfully theirs; that is, in terms of the failure to respect the unencumbered choices of persons. However, not all failures to respect unencumbered choice constitute harm; only failures to respect such choice within a certain sphere amount to harm. Thus, the understanding of harm requires that we attend to the problem of what this sphere is.

How might we define the sphere in which a person's own choice must prevail? This is essentially a problem of deciding to whom various decisions should be assigned. Who should have control of this and who of that? The ethics of respect for persons handles this problem by making an assignment of control indicated by its basic commitment. That is, control over each person is assigned by the ethics of respect for persons to *that* person. This is, I take it, clearly indicated by the claim that each person should have control over his or her own life. The difficulty with this is that there are sometimes disputes as to whose life something is a part of, and that some things seem to be part of more than one person's life. But let us return to these difficulties later. The immediate problem is one of understanding what it is for a person to have control over herself in the way required by respect for persons. Four aspects of personal control may readily be identified.

First, control over a person's own body is assigned by respect-for-persons ethics to the person whose body it is. Insofar as anyone makes things happen to or with a particular person's body, it should be done by that person or with that person's unencumbered consent. Thus, one way of harming a person is to make something happen to or with the person's body without the person's actual or hypothetical unencumbered consent.

Second, respect-for-persons ethics also requires that a person's mental/ psychological processes and characteristics — I shall refer to these as 'mentation'[12] — not be altered without the person's unencumbered consent. This provision rules out the making of modifications in a person's character, beliefs, values, interests, and so on, by means which do not give the person the opportunity to make an unencumbered choice as to whether to accept or resist the change. 'Mind control' thus counts as one form of harm.[13]

Third, we have a classification which is perhaps implicit in the first two, but which is so important that it deserves separate mention. The decision as to what actions or activities a person shall engage in is also a decision assigned by respect-for-persons ethics to the individual person. The decision as to what a particular individual shall do should be made by that individual. Forcing a person to do something and preventing a person from doing something are thus forms of harm. Included here are both physical interference with action and the use of threats of imposition of other wrongs to influence action.

Fourth, one's sphere of control must extend still further, for crimes such as theft cannot be accounted for as deprivations of control over one's body, mentation, or liberty of action. Control over things in the world other than persons is not easily assigned.[14] However, control over things in the world is sometimes assigned to particular persons through conventional arrangements.

These *conventional assignments* of control may occur with varying degrees of formality. The legal contracts through which one may acquire control of real property are highly formal, while methods of purchase through which one may acquire control of personal property, e.g., clothing, are less so. The nature of the conventions, of course, may vary widely from time to time and from place to place. Where control over objects is conventionally assigned, that assignment must normally be respected, since interference with the objects assigned to an individual's control could so easily be interference with her chosen projects.

These four aspects of personal control represent major components of what I shall refer to as one's *personal sphere*. This sphere is composed of that over which one may rightfully exert unilateral control and with which it is *prima facie* wrong for others to interfere. The test of whether something is part of a person's personal sphere is an appeal to the principle of respect for persons. Something is part of one's personal sphere just when assignment of unilateral control over the thing to individuals best reflects the commitment to the importance of everyone's having control over his or her own life. Allowing each person to have unilateral control over his or her own body, mentation, choice of actions, and conventionally assigned objects best reflects this commitment because any other assignment would leave persons less able to conduct lives of their own choosing. The *prima facie* right to unilateral control over these aspects of oneself is essential to any conception of persons' having control over their own lives. This, I trust, is intuitively plausible enough that I may defer discussion of some possible alternative assignments of control to a later section.[15]

This makes possible a respect-for-persons understanding of harm as that concept is to be used in conjunction with the harm principle. To harm someone is to use or alter his or her personal sphere without his/her unencumbered empirical consent. It is, in other words, to make things happen in a sphere in which things should be made to happen only by that person or with the unencumbered agreement of that person. A few additional explanatory remarks will help to clarify this proposal.

Under the harm principle, harm is a matter of *making things happen* in someone's personal sphere; harm is thus a result only of positive *actions* as opposed to *omissions*. This approach is adopted largely as a matter of convenience. The harm principle is the one principle of legal coercion which is relatively uncontroversial; this uncontroversial character of the principle can be preserved only if it is not taken to include omissions which could prevent bad consequences. Thus, on the present approach, the harm principle is designed to cover only positive actions which violate the sphere in which persons are to have unilateral control. More controversial uses of coercive law are discussed under the headings of other possible principles. This, of course, means that the harm principle does not necessarily identify all acceptable uses of law.

It is perhaps also worth emphasizing that the conception of harm used in conjunction with the harm principle is not necessarily identical with the general use of that concept. As indicated earlier, the interests conception of harm may in some form best approximate the general use of 'harm'. A theory of the proper uses of law, however, needs a conception of harm which identifies enforceable requirements, and thus uses a narrower conception of harm. The present approach takes it as given that positive actions which may be interfered with because of the way they affect others shall be deemed harmful, and uses the principle of respect for persons to identify which actions these are. Use of the term 'harm' is not really essential, but has been adopted here because its use in this context is so well entrenched. Thus, my analysis of 'harm' is applicable only to the narrower use.

Most of the things people do cannot correctly be described as making something happen to or with another's person or property. Writing a letter, painting a house, digging a trench, attending a play, and many other activities do not make things happen in the personal spheres of others. Even many activities which do involve others do not make things happen to them without their cooperation, and thus are not equivalent to taking control from them. So one may play chess with someone, wrestle with someone, have sexual intercourse with someone without depriving them of control, and thus what one does is not making something happen to them (so to speak) unilaterally. Their willing participation in the activity prevents it from being a case of violating their personal spheres.

When things are made to happen within the personal spheres of others, the boundaries of acceptable action have been crossed. Thus, the murderer violates the standards of respect-for-persons ethics because the act of murder makes something happen to the body of another without the latter's willing cooperation. The decision of when the victim will die, insofar as it should be made by anyone, must be made by the victim, not someone else. Something which should be made to happen only by one person, is made to happen by someone else, and that makes the latter's action unacceptable. In this way, the wrongness of acts of violence may be accounted for. Physical attacks, including rape, involve making something happen to a person which should happen, if at all, only with the willing participation of that person. The common element in these wrongs is the taking from persons of choices which should be theirs alone. There will, of course, be widely varying degrees of seriousness of harm once this threshold is crossed as well as (in many cases) associated psychological harm, but the unifying element remains the invasion of the personal sphere.

In addition to providing an account of violent harm and theft (the violation of conventional assignments of control), this conception of harm also accords well with certain other uses of the notion of harm related to the harm principle. For instance, a person may be harmed without ever knowing it,[16] and some conceptions of harm have difficulty accounting for this. The present view, however, allows for this. Suppose that Jack takes Dave's car late one night, uses it for two hours, and then returns it without Dave ever noticing that it was gone. Dave has been harmed in a way that should be covered by the harm principle, and the present view provides for this in that Jack's action involves taking control of something assigned to Dave's control. Whatever is done with Dave's car should be decided by Dave, and since Jack has not respected this requirement, he has violated Dave's personal sphere.

This account of harm also provides a place for the maxim *Volenti non fit injuria.*[17] On the view of harm here defended, there is a sense in which it is true that a person is not harmed by that to which he or she consents. There is a qualification to this, of course, in that the consent must be unencumbered, but since harm has been defined in terms of the taking of control from others, no harm occurs if those involved retain control over that which is assigned to them by their unencumbered cooperation in what takes place. On the aforementioned wider conception of harm, the concept is not so qualified. For instance, even persons who know the dangers of smoking may be said to be *harming* themselves by that activity. However, if we keep in mind that we are approaching this from the perspective of a moral theory which which takes persons' control over their own lives as of primary importance, the appropriateness of the *Volenti* provision is apparent.

Let us now return to a problem set aside earlier, viz, the way in which the personal spheres of different individuals may seem to overlap. The problem derives from the claim that each person must be allowed to determine for him/herself what actions he/she shall perform. Does this mean that we cannot interfere with Jack, say, if he decides to rape Linda? Of course it does not, and the explanation of this is that it is only *prima facie* wrong to interfere with someone's personal sphere. That is, invasion of someone's personal sphere is wrong unless there are special features of a particular invasion which make it acceptable even in light of its being an invasion of someone's personal sphere. To say that something is *prima facie* wrong is to say that it is wrong under a description which may not include all the morally relevant features of particular cases which fall under the description; some cases wrong under an incomplete description will not be wrong, all things considered. In respect-for-persons ethics, these will be cases in which interference with someone's personal sphere best respects the commitment to everyone's having control over his or her own life. The principles of legal coercion developed in the present work identify the most important circumstances in which that is the case. In the rape case, the fact that Jack's chosen action makes use of something within Linda's personal sphere (her body), means that his action is harmful, *prima facie* wrong, and wrong all things considered unless there is something about the particular case of overriding importance. Further, others (e.g., Linda, the police, etc.) would be justified in interfering with Jack, despite the fact that this is *prima facie* wrong, because of the special features of this case of interference. In part, this simply means that respect-for-persons ethics incorporates the commonplace view that one's right to freely choose one's actions is limited to actions not violative of other persons.

It is now possible to provide a statement of the version of the harm principle required by the principle of respect for persons. The *harm principle* is the following:

> It is not a violation of the principle of respect for persons to use coercive law to prevent persons from performing actions which violate the personal spheres of other persons.

Primary components of one's personal sphere, again, are one's body, one's mentation, one's choice of actions, and things conventionally assigned to one's control. This sphere is violated when what is in it is used or altered by others without one's unencumbered consent.

It is important that the personal sphere not be confused with the *protected* sphere (cf. Section 2.2). The personal sphere is the sphere invasion of which, whether by law or by individual action, is *prima facie* wrong. The principles of legal coercion identify circumstances under which law may interfere with the personal spheres of persons. The *protected sphere* is the realm in which there is no justification for legal interference with the personal spheres of persons; the protected sphere, in other words, is the sphere in which legal intervention is wrong not only *prima facie*, but all things considered. What cannot be brought under the principles of legal coercion lies in the protected sphere.

CHAPTER FOUR

LEGAL PATERNALISM

4.1. THE PRINCIPLE OF PATERNALISM

The harm principle permits the use of legal coercion in some cases in which an individual's actions are not confined to the sphere in which his or her choices must be respected; when an individual's actions are so confined, another principle is especially relevant — that of paternalism. A paternalistic action is an action which involves doing something which is *prima facie* wrong to a person for the reason that the action is believed to be for the overall good of that person despite its wrongful aspects.[1] The principle of paternalism authorizes some uses of coercive law which cannot be brought under the harm principle.

Consider some of the (not necessarily legal) cases about which there seems to be agreement that paternalistic interventions can be justified. Perhaps the most obvious case in which it seems intuitively clear that paternalism may be justified is that which gives paternalism its name: the case of children. When children get themselves in situations which are likely to be harmful to them, the use of force to prevent them from being harmed seems quite reasonable; in some cases, the failure to protect them from themselves may be quite monstrous (e.g., the child is about to touch a wire which carries a potentially fatal current). More problematic are cases in which children are coerced in order to obtain for them some benefit rather than to protect them from some harm. But even here, some paternalism (e.g., compulsory education) is widely accepted. And presumably the justification for the paternalistic coercion of children lies in the apparent fact that children do not always understand the harms to which they may be subject and the potential benefits which they may miss.

A second sort of case which seems to be fairly non-controversial is that in which someone acts in ignorance of some fact or facts which would be very likely to be considered by him to be highly relevant to what he is doing. For example, consider John Doe, standing on a hill in the path of a runaway automobile. Surely a passerby could be justified in pushing him out of danger, for he would surely move himself if only he were aware of the threat. Or if Doe is about to light a match, unaware that it will cause an explosion, few would deny that someone could be justified in preventing his action, even if Doe alone would be injured by it. Again, an important aspect of the situation is the fact that Doe is ignorant of some relevant fact which is known to the person who would perform the paternalistic coercion.

Another sort of case would be that which someone makes a decision or undertakes an action while under great emotional stress. John Doe tries to slash his wrists after a week in which his son dies of a heroin overdose, his wife leaves him, his house burns down, and he is fired from his job. An extreme example perhaps, but of course the point is that Doe is doing something under stressful conditions which may cause him to make decisions he would not otherwise make. If the consequences of his action are serious enough, paternalistic interventions could possibly be justified.

Cases in which a person's choice is compelled provide other examples. If, for some reason, John Doe is compelled to do something which is harmful to himself, then someone else might be justified in intervening to prevent Doe from doing it. The compulsion could be of various sorts, ranging, perhaps, from brain malfunction through neurotic compulsion to strong temptation.[2] But whatever its source or nature, it may be that Doe would decide differently were it not for the compulsion, and, perhaps for that reason, it may be justifiable to intervene.

A type of case which is closely related to compulsion cases is that in which a person does something possibly harmful to himself because he has been subjected to *undue influence*. C. L. Ten cites[3] the quaint example of a South Rhodesian air-hostess who consented to being caned by her employer rather than lose her job or her flight pay for violation of company regulations. The woman would presumably not have consented to such a thing had she not been subjected to the threat of loss of pay. According to Ten, the employer was convicted of assault. At least part of the motivation for intervention in such cases could be paternalistic.

Yet another category is that of the mentally ill, insane, or irrational. Persons who are categorized as mentally ill may behave in ways which are self-destructive; suppose, for example, that someone tries to chop up his own arm with a butcher knife while believing that he is cutting up a piece of meat. Here the fact that the person believes something which is so obviously false provides some reason for regarding him as irrational or, perhaps, mentally ill. As an irrational or mentally ill person, he may not understand what he is doing to himself, and someone who finds him about to engage in self-destructive behavior would seem to be justified in intervening.

Also relevant here are cases in which a person who is not known to fall into one of the above categories is about to do something which will cause him severe and irreversible harm. For example, the person is about to do something which will cause his death or serious bodily injury. Here the mere fact that the person is about to cause himself severe and irreversible harm may be taken as sufficient to justify intervention. At least, someone might be justified in preventing the infliction of the harm long enough to determine whether the person inflicting the harm on himself falls into any of the other categories.

Finally, there is the sort of case which may be described as that of the *non-rational* person.[4] This is the sort of person who is not able to make decisions or choices at all and who therefore is unable to act on any decision. For example, suppose that John Doe has been knocked unconscious in an accident. He is therefore unable to make a decision about whether or not to allow himself to be taken to a hospital, but it seems plausible to suppose that someone would be justified in taking him there although the reason for doing so would be largely or entirely paternalistic. This case, of course, is one in which the person is protected not so much from what he does *to* himself, but from what he cannot do *for* himself.

What is common to most of these cases is that the action or failure to act of the person treated paternalistically is *encumbered* (see Section 1.6). Action under ignorance, emotional stress, compulsion, undue influence, mental illness, and similar conditions is action likely to be influenced by error-causing conditions, and is thus encumbered. So, too, is the failure to act of the person non-rational due to lack of consciousness. Now intervention in these cases gives the appearance of being in violation of the principle of respect for persons, either because a person is prevented from doing what he or she has chosen or because something is done to or for the person which should only be done by the person's own choice. But since the actions (including failures to act) here in question are encumbered, the demands of respect for persons are not necessarily violated, for those demands call for deference to the *unencumbered* choices of persons.

The question then arises of how one treats persons as persons when dealing with someone whose action is encumbered. The answer is that one attempts to treat the person in accordance with his or her *unencumbered* choices insofar as they can be ascertained. This approach gives rise to the following standard for the identification of justifiable cases of paternalism. The *principle of paternalism:*

Paternalistic interventions do not violate the principle of respect for persons if and only if (i) there is good evidence that the decisions with respect to which the person is to be coerced are encumbered, and (ii) there is good evidence that this person's decisions would be supportive of the paternalistic intervention if they were not encumbered.[5]

Let us consider some of the important concepts included in this principle.

Good Evidence

The principle of paternalism relies on the same concept of good evidence as that used in any other area in which rational support for assertions is required. In general, evidence for a claim may be considered good evidence when it is factually correct and it serves as the premise or premises of a non-fallacious inductive or deductive argument in which the claim serves as the conclusion. Thus, if the argument is deductive, good evidence is provided only if the argument is valid and the premises are true. If the argument is inductive and its premises are true, the evidence provided is only as good as the strength of the inductive argument. Since the strength of inductive arguments varies in degree, the strength of the evidence for an inductively supported conclusion can also vary in degree. Also relevant to the value of an inductive argument is the question of whether there is also evidence which supports claims incompatible with the conclusion of the argument. Evidence would not count as good evidence for a claim if an incompatible conclusion is supported by a stronger argument. These features of inductive argument are especially important for paternalism, for much of the crucial evidence in its justification is empirical and thus depends ultimately on inductive reasoning.

Decisions Supportive of Intervention

The principle of paternalism allows intervention only when the hypothetical unencumbered decisions of the person to be coerced are *supportive of* the intervention. This means that if the person were not in the encumbered circumstance, he would expressly consent to the intervention. Thus, if there is good evidence that the person, when in an unencumbered state, would agree that if he were in circumstances of the sort in question, he should be, and would want to be, subjected to paternalistic coercion, then that person's decisions may be said to be supportive of internvention.

Hypothetical Unencumbered Decisions

The justification of intervention requires that the intervening party have some information as to what the person's decisions or choices *would be if* they were not encumbered. Sometimes this information is not difficult to obtain. Suppose that White is about to take a drink of poisoned wine not knowing that it is poisoned. White's good friend Black, who knows that the wine is poisoned and that White does not know it, must consider whether to intervene. Suppose that Black has every reason to believe that White has no intention of doing away with himself: White, let us suppose, has expressed no such intention; on the contrary, he has expressed the intention of carrying out a wide variety of plans in the future. Under such circumstances, Black surely has good evidence that White would choose not to drink the wine if he knew it was poisoned, and that Black would support intervention to prevent him from doing so in the encumbered circumstance. Thus, according to the principle of paternalism, Black's intervention would be justified.

The unique feature of the case of Black and White is the fact that the prediction about White's hypothetical unencumbered decisions can easily be verified. Black intervenes, tells White that the drink is poisoned, and then if White expresses no further desire to drink the wine and no objection to the intervention, Black's prediction is verified. In this case verification is not difficult to obtain because the encumbrance of White's decision – ignorance of the fact that the wine is poisoned – is fairly easily removed.

Other cases are more problematic. Sometimes an intervening party, unlike Black in the above example, will have no personal information about the person to be coerced. In such cases, prediction of the hypothetical unencumbered will is more difficult. In general, the smaller the quantity of information about the person to be coerced that is available to the intervening party, the more difficult it will be to make accurate predictions about the former's decisions in the absence of the encumbrance. Another factor which serves to make accurate predictions difficult is the nature of the encumbrance involved. When a person is ignorant of one relevant fact about what he is doing, as in the case of the poisoned wine, it is relatively easy to predict what effect the elimination of the ignorance will have on the person's decisions. However, when the encumbrance is something like emotional stress or possibly mental illness, it is much more difficult to predict the effect of the removal of the encumbrance. If, for instance, the case involves someone who has been mentally retarded all of his life, it would be impossible to make detailed predictions as to what his views would be with any great accuracy. Thus, both the lack of clear-cut information about the effect of removal of the encumbrance and the lack of personal information about the party to be coerced, are factors contributing to inaccuracy in the making of predictions as to the nature of a person's hypothetical unencumbered decisions.

The determination of a person's hypothetical unencumbered decisions requires, however, that all information which may have a bearing on these decisions be taken into account. This includes information about the person's goals, beliefs, and values, and also information about the probable effects of various forms of encumbrance on a person's decisions. Much of the information required, therefore, is of an empirical nature and is thus subject to the difficulties of making accurate predictions on the basis of empirical evidence. The question of whether a given act of paternalism is justified may thus often be in doubt due to the uncertainty of the prediction about the person's hypothetical unencumbered decisions.

One final factor which will frequently figure in the identification of acceptable cases of paternalism is seen in examples like those mentioned above in which someone is protected from a threat of serious harm. However, the existence of a threat of serious harm does not in itself constitute an encumbrance, nor does it serve as a necessary or sufficient condition of justified intervention. Instead, the presence of a threat of serious harm functions as *evidence* of the satisfaction of conditions necessary for justified paternalism. This is because the threat of serious harm may provide evidence both that an encumbrance is present and that the person's unencumbered decision would support intervention. It might provide evidence of encumbrance because the presence of encumbrance may be a likely explanation of why the person is about to harm himself or herself. The person may not be aware of the threat. The threat of serious harm constitutes evidence that a person's hypothetical unencumbered decisions would be supportive of paternalistic intervention because of the fact that virtually everyone wishes to avoid serious harm virtually all of the time; so someone threatened with such harm is likely to support intervention. Of course, in both of these cases the threat of harm is not conclusive evidence that the respective conditions are satisfied, since facts about the particular cases in question may provide more compelling evidence to the contrary.

4.2. PATERNALISM AND LAW

With this general understanding of the respect-for-persons approach to paternalism, let us next consider specifically *legal* paternalism. In terms of straightforward application of the principle of paternalism, it is clear that it will be difficult to make out a paternalistic case for the prohibition of many kinds of conduct. Consider the possibility of prohibiting smoking on paternalistic grounds. In order for such a prohibition to be justified, it would have to be shown, first, that everyone who smokes does so with an encumbered will, and, second, that everyone would support the prohibition if able to assess the question free of encumbrance. There is every reason to think that neither of these conditions is satisfied. Even if some persons smoke because of a kind of psychological compulsion which would constitute encumbrance, not all do. And even if the encumbrance condition were satisfied, there is ample evidence that not everyone would support the intervention if unencumbered in the fact that some persons under no encumbrance (e.g., non-smokers aware of the facts about smoking) oppose such prohibitions. Similar things may be said about other seemingly paternalistic legislation proposed or adopted in recent years. Requiring motorcyclists to wear helmets and automobile drivers and passengers to wear seat belts fails to treat persons as persons because of the unencumbered choices of many persons to risk going without these forms of protection and to oppose these requirements.

What the principle of paternalism does clearly permit is the possibility of paternalistic interventions done on a case-by-case basis. That is, even if prohibition or requirement of general kinds of conduct is not possible under the principle of paternalism, that does not rule out the possibility that paternalism may be justified in specific cases. If, for instance, a court were to consider the circumstances of a particular individual, it might find that the conditions imposed by the principle of paternalism were satisfied. In such cases, paternalistic intervention could be justified.

An example of a case which was decided in a manner roughly as required by the principle of paternalism is *Superintendent of Belchertown v. Saikewicz*.[6] Saikewicz was a sixty-seven-year-old man described as being profoundly mentally retarded and unable to communicate verbally. He was suffering from a form of leukemia, and the question to be decided was whether to permit this condition to be treated with chemotherapy or to allow it to go untreated. The use of chemotherapy was considered questionable mainly because it would have involved painful side effects, a low probability of producing any substantial improvement in the patient's condition, and would not have been understood by the patient. Despite its drawbacks, however, most patients for whom chemotherapy is the medically indicated treatment reportedly do elect to receive it.

This case may be considered an instance of legal paternalism because in it the court takes upon itself a decision — whether or not to treat Saikewicz with chemotherapy — which ideally should be made by Saikewicz himself and because it is assumed that whatever is decided will be done for his own good. The first condition of the principle of paternalism is clearly met in this case since Saikewicz's own thinking on this choice (if any) is encumbered by his profound retardation. Therefore, under the principle of paternalism, what should guide the decision of the court is a determination of the hypothetical unencumbered will of the patient. As we have seen, this calls for a judgment as to what the individual would choose if able to make a choice about the situation in question while not subject to any encumbrance.

The reasoning of the *Saikewicz* court is in many respects just what is called for by the principle of paternalism. First, the court "take[s] the view that the substantive rights of the competent and the incompetent persons are the same in regard to the right to decline potentially life-prolonging treatment".[7] To begin with anything other than the view that the fundamental rights of competents and incompetents are the same would be to deny personhood to one of these classes. Their differences are properly taken into account only when the question becomes that of what respecting their status as persons requires in particular circumstances. For both, respect for persons requires that we be guided by respect for unencumbered choice; for competents (the unencumbered) that means respect for empirical choice, and for incompetents (the encumbered) that means deference to hypothetical unencumbered choice. We cannot rule out in advance the possibility that either will sometimes reject potentially life-prolonging treatment.

Second, the court acknowledges the relevance of judgments as to what most competent persons would decide to do in similar circumstances: "[e]vidence that most people would or would not act in a certain way is certainly an important consideration in attempting to ascertain the predilections of any individual".[8] Such evidence is especially appropriate in cases such as that of Saikewicz where nothing is known of the individual's unencumbered preferences. That fact that most persons would have a given preference provides some evidence that a specific individual would as well; indeed, there may often be nothing else to go on.

Third, and most importantly, the court asserts that the decisive factor in rendering its decision should be "the unique perspective of the person called on to make the decision".[9] The court's "goal is to determine with as much accuracy as possible the wants and needs of the individual involved".[10] This is to recognize that while what most persons would do is relevant, the judgment of others must give way to the judgment of the individual in question. Only in this way are his unencumbered choices respected and only in this way is he treated fully as a person. Thus, if something is known about the particular individual or his circumstances which shows that he would choose differently from others, that is decisive. In *Saikewicz*, the court concludes that a patient would not choose to undergo suffering not understood by the patient for the sake of a merely modest chance of not very substantial benefits. It therefore rules against chemotherapy for Saikewicz. In basing its decision on the attempt to ascertain what the particular individual involved would say about the alternatives, the court has approached the case in the manner called for by the principle of paternalism.

Cases involving blood transfusions for Jehovah's Witnesses may also be illustrative. A relatively simple instance of this would be that of a Jehovah's Witness who, after calm deliberation and with full awareness of the consequences, refuses to consent to a transfusion clearly necessary to sustain life. It might be argued here that this choice *is* encumbered, in that it is influenced by a false belief that there is a god who disapproves of blood transfusions. Even if this is accepted, however, there remains the question of whether the individual would allow such a belief to be overridden even if false. Because of the indignity involved in having *this* sort of belief overridden, and because the individual is aware of the consequences of adhering to the belief, evidence that such a person's hypothetical unencumbered judgments would support intervention is lacking. The principle of paternalism therefore would not permit the forced transfusion under these circumstances.

Compare the case of an accident victim who needs a transfusion to live, but who is also a Jehovah's Witness. Suppose this person is unconscious and it has not been possible to locate anyone who knows her personally. All that is known is that she is a member of Jehovah's Witnesses; nothing is known about her views specifically on the blood transfusion doctrine. The victim's failure to consent to the transfusion is clearly encumbered, since she is unconscious, so the only issue is the determination of her hypothetical unencumbered will. Here the correct decision under the principle of paternalism would be to go ahead with the transfusion. The only reason not to is that the victim is a member of a *group* which does not believe in transfusions. This evidence is outweighed by two factors. First, we know that it is not uncommon for persons who have membership in religious and other organizations to reject specific aspects of the official doctrine of the organization (e.g., Catholics who practice birth control). Second, we know that virtually everyone cares very much about life, and that it is not uncommon for people to do things they would not ordinarily do in order to preserve their lives (e.g., killing in self-defense). Thus, it seems reasonable to assume that the victim is more likely to approve hypothetically of the transfusion than not.[11]

Some interesting possibilities are raised by a third Jehovah's Witness case. Suppose that the patient, again a Jehovah's Witness who requires a blood transfusion to live, responds to the request that she consent to it by saying that her religious beliefs do not permit such consent, but that if a court orders the transfusion without her consent, the responsibility will not be hers.[12] The implication is that she wants the court to order the transfusion without her consent. She wants both to live and to honor her religious beliefs. If the court orders the transfusion, she gets that because she is not responsible for the transfusion being done.

The principle of paternalism would permit the transfusion in this case. The patient's failure to consent is encumbered by special circumstances which make her unable to express her true wish. The very expression of her true desire would prevent it from being obtained. Since the decision not to consent is influenced by a factor which will cause that decision to have consequences the patient wants to avoid, it is an encumbered decision. If it were not for the self-defeating nature of the patient's expression of her true desire (i.e., absent the encumbrance), she would express the desire that the transfusion be performed without her empirical consent (i.e., her hypothetical unencumbered will supports the intervention). In this way, the principle of paternalism could permit transfusions of Jehovah's Witnesses without their consent. Care must be taken, of course, that cases such as these are not confused with cases like the first in which there is no unexpressable desire that the transfusion be done without consent. In the absence of other complications (e.g., unconsciousness), these cases presumably would often be distinguished by the way in which the patient refuses to consent. A patient who says that he or she wants not to have the transfusion or who attempts physically to resist having it performed would appear to be in a class with our first Jehovah's Witness, while a patient who says only that he or she cannot give *consent* for the transfusion, or cannot take responsibility for it, appears to be in a class with our third.

CHAPTER FIVE

THE WELFARE PRINCIPLE

5.1. INTRODUCTION

The harm principle and the principle of paternalism provide defenses for only a limited range of possible legislation. One kind of legislation which does not appear to be defensible under those principles is legislation requiring persons to aid others in need or to provide benefits to others. The principle of paternalism clearly would not warrant such laws, and the harm principle has been restricted to cover actions and not omissions. Thus, it is doubtful whether any basis has been provided for what may be called welfare legislation; the possibility of defending such legislation demands specific consideration.

5.2. THE BASIS OF POSITIVE RIGHTS

The harm principle expresses what must be one of the least controversial moral judgments that can be made, viz, that it is acceptable to interfere with individuals' attempts to harm others. We have seen that that claim has a foundation in the principle of respect for persons; recognition of the special moral status of persons requires that they not be harmed, and this means that they must be allowed to live lives of their own choosing. What is of fundamental importance, therefore, is that persons be able to live lives of their own choosing. This is important enough that the way persons behave in regard to other persons must be limited so as to make this possible.

The possibility of welfare legislation raises the question of just how the implications of this basic principle are to be specified. Here the question is whether recognition of the special moral status of persons entails a moral requirement to aid others, or merely the moral requirement not to harm others actively. We might gain some insight into what is involved in acting consistently with recognition of something as *important* by considering cases of other things thought to have an importance worthy of restricting human action. Many persons believe, for instance, that the continued existence of certain things in nature, such as redwood forests, would be of importance;

53

many others believe that the preservation of great works of art would be of value. One consequence of these judgments is that those who make them believe that they ought not perform actions which will destroy the things believed to be of special importance. The defender of the redwoods will take care to put out her campfires fully when visiting forests, and the owner of valued art treasures will be certain not to handle them in ways that will damage them. One who recognizes the importance of these things feels an obligation to take the care necessary to see that he or she does them no damage. But surely that is not all that is called for by the judgment that these things are of importance. Our camper will also be willing to put out smoldering fires left by others, and the art collector will take steps to ensure that his works are not harmed by, e.g., excessive exposure to sunlight or moisture.

Actions of this last type are not merely actions which avoid harming the things judged to have a special status, but are positive actions taken to protect these things from dangers regardless of their source. Are these actions *required* by the view that the things in question are of special importance? Well, would not the failure to protect these special things belie the claim that they are thought to be of such importance? We do not merely refrain from destroying the things we value; we also protect them from dangers other than ourselves. And in general, does not the claim that something is of value imply that we ought to protect it from dangers in general and not merely from destruction at our own hands?

If, then, the prohibition against harming other persons is an expression of the view that it is of supreme moral importance that persons live lives of their own choosing, is there not also reason to recognize positive moral requirements to aid others in some circumstances? Recognition of the importance of persons would seem to require more than merely leaving them alone. To passively permit the death of someone who wants to live and could be saved at little cost must be to fail to attribute to that person any real worth. It is certainly to fail to attribute *supreme* worth to persons if persons are allowed to die when they could be saved in ways that do not threaten the existence of other equally worthy beings. Consider what we would say of someone who claimed to recognize the supreme importance of persons, but who was unwilling to take even costless steps to prevent a person's death. The failure to act in that sort of case could not be rendered consistent with the supposed recognition of the moral importance of persons as a guide to action. We would simply not believe the man who claimed to accept the importance of persons while failing to prevent a person's death when that could be done at no cost.

One way in which an opponent of positive moral requirements might attempt to prevent this inference from negative rights and duties to positive rights and duties by means of the principle underlying the negative rights, would be to postulate the negative principle as the fundamental principle. That is, one might insist that the fundamental moral principle is just the one which says that there are negative duties to respect the negative rights of persons. This would be to say that persons have (so to speak) moral fences built around them which establish moral boundaries, and that moral wrongs consist in violations of these boundaries — unjustified boundary-crossings, as it were.[1] If such a principle were the fundamental one, there would, of course, be no basis for the inference to positive moral requirements.

The objection to this move is that it begs the question. Whether such a principle is the fundamental one is what is at issue. Further, it seems legitimate to ask the question of *why* these boundaries should not be crossed, why the fences should be respected. Unless we may seek some more fundamental principle, it is difficult to see how the issue between positive and negative moral requirements could be dealt with. However, it seems that the only plausible explanations of the wrongness of the boundary-crossing also provide a basis for positive requirements. The Kantian approach adopted in the present study does provide this in saying that the fences should be respected because it is of the greatest moral importance that persons live lives of their own choosing. If what is behind the fence is important enough that we ought to detour to avoid crossing it, then should it not also be taken as important enough that we should sometimes take positive action to protect it when it is threatened from sources other than ourselves? The moral importance of persons seems to entail both positive and negative requirements.[2]

5.3. THE PLAUSIBILITY OF POSITIVE RIGHTS

Why would anyone be led to deny this conclusion? A main reason for the advocacy of merely negative rights has to do with the assumption that positive rights would impose requirements that are too stringent, that recognition of such rights would require the judgment that many omissions we generally regard as innocent are really morally wrong, and that therefore the realm of liberty left to persons would be too severely restricted. A related concern is that recognition of positive rights would render inappropriate the way in which we regard assisting others as praiseworthy, as deserving of reward, and as supererogatory. There is also the view that recognition of a positive right to life would mean that there is no moral difference between killing and letting die, and that therefore such actions as the killing of one person to prevent the deaths of several others would be found permissible or even required. Since the main objections to positive rights have to do with these implications for individuals, we shall have to spend some time on these problems before developing a view about positive rights and legal coercion.

The liberty-based objection to positive rights may be formulated as a concern about the fact that positive rights do restrict the liberty of those upon whom the burden of acting in response to them falls. Being required to act in the manner demanded by a positive right, one is not at liberty to do as one chooses. Clearly, however, the mere fact that a proposed moral requirement restricts a person's right to act as she chooses cannot be a decisive objection to the requirement. If it were, there could be no requirements not to act in ways that harm others, since those requirements also restrict choice. But, as was noted above, if the continuation of the ability of persons to control their lives through their own choices is important enough to justify restraint on our liberty to perform positive actions, why is it not also important enough to require other positive actions? The basis of the restriction on liberty is the same in both cases: actions (including omissions) of certain kinds are inconsistent with recognition of the moral importance of persons' being able to live lives of their own choosing. No non-arbitrary, non-question-begging way of explaining why we should be concerned, as this objection supposes, only with not interfering with others presents itself. The mere fact that positive rights may restrict liberty need not be taken as a serious matter. If any liberty-based objection to positive rights should concern us, it must be an objection based not simply on the presence of a restriction on liberty, but on the *extent* of the restriction involved. Positive rights may be thought to involve such extensive interferences with liberty as to be unacceptable.

To evaluate this second version of the liberty-based objection, we need to consider further what must be involved in the recognition of positive rights. Some ways of formulating positive rights could involve excessive demands, but this is not entailed by the notion of positive rights itself. Rights to assistance based on the moral status of persons involve a number of limitations which undermine the force of this objection. For one thing, rights to assistance impose actual obligations or duties on others only if what is needed cannot be provided by the needy person himself. If the person in question is capable of getting what he needs for himself without difficulty, but willfully and without encumbrance fails to do so, then *he* has chosen his own fate and the failure of others to provide for him is not a failure to respect his status as a person. To require others to provide assistance which a person could easily provide for himself would be to allow the latter excessive control over others; he could require others to do things for him simply by refusing to do them for himself, and that kind of willful control of one person over others is inconsistent with the others' rights to determine their own lives. This limitation is important, for the failure to recognize it seems to lie behind much controversy concerning the providing of assistance. For example, much opposition to welfare seems to rest on the denial that those who receive aid really need it.

In addition, there must be strict limits on the extent of the sacrifice which others may be *required* to make in order to provide assistance. No one should be required to sacrifice his own status as a person in order to provide assistance to others. To require that would be to sacrifice one person for the sake of another, a requirement that would not be consistent with the basis of rights to assistance, i.e., that of the supreme status of each person. A person sacrificed for the sake of another is not recognized as having the kind of supreme worth implied by that notion. Thus, rights to assistance require assistance only when assistance can be provided without sacrificing other persons. Accordingly, the killing of one person to save others would not be permitted on this view.[3]

A further limitation on rights to assistance lies in the circumstances in which one is required to provide aid. If there is at this moment a patient in a hospital in Hong Kong who requires artificial respiration in order to live, an attending physician who fails to provide this assistance has allowed the patient to die in a way which violates the patient's right to life. A man in London who knows nothing of the case and has no reason to know of it, has not. A right to assistance imposes requirements only on those who have the capacity and the opportunity to provide assistance.

These limitations on rights to assistance are intended to show that recognition of such rights does not necessarily entail moral reassessment of the perhaps universal failure of human beings to use every means to satisfy every need of their fellows. The failure to use extreme means to discover and to assist others in need is not a violation of the positive right to life based on the moral status of persons. But there is still a question about the cases in which positive rights do impose demands on others to provide assistance: we often regard those who provide assistance as having done something more than is morally required, and as therefore praiseworthy and deserving of reward in a way not appropriate to those who merely do not violate others' rights. If persons have some rights to assistance, how can those who provide the assistance properly be regarded as meritorious in these ways?

Part of the explanation of this phenomenon no doubt lies in the fact that rights to assistance do not extend to cases of the sort just discussed, while many cases of providing aid are of that sort, so that the assistance is not in response to a right. However, I want to suggest that even in cases in which those assisted have a right to assistance, there is a place for notions of supererogation and reward. Consider some features of positive rights. Unlike a negative right to life, which is respected only if *everyone refrains* from performing actions which would endanger the rightholder's life, a positive right to life closes off options not closed by a negative right to life only when someone with a positive right actually needs assistance. When no positive rightbearer actually needs assistance, the existence of positive rights closes off no additional options to others, while when such a rightbearer does need assistance, the option of failing to provide assistance is foreclosed. But even in this case the demands of the right to assistance are not parallel to the demands of the negative right to life, for the right to assistance does not as such require anything of *everyone*; the right to assistance is respected so long as *someone* provides the assistance. If anyone does provide the needed assistance, then others continue to have no options closed to them, just as in the case in which assistance is not needed.

This aspect of rights to assistance raises the further problem that rights to assistance as such do not specify on whom the obligation to provide assistance falls. Negative rights impose an obligation of restraint on everyone, but since not everyone need act in order to provide needed assistance, the burdens imposed by rights to assistance do not necessarily fall on everyone and may fall on no one in particular. A wide variety of cases could occur in this connection. Some such cases seem to impose obligations on someone, but not any particular person, and not even every person in a similar situation. The drowning man at the beach, for instance, could be saved if only one of the twenty persons nearby would throw him a life preserver, but which of them should do it? None has a special obligation to provide aid to this person, and yet it would not do to have all twenty fighting over the life preserver while our drowning friend goes down for the last time. Thus, we could say that each person has an obligation to provide assistance, but only so long as the assistance is needed; then, if someone else gets to the life preserver first, providing the needed aid, the obligation of others ceases.

I submit that the difference between cases of this kind and cases of negative rights is sufficient to account for the feeling that there is something optional or supererogatory about providing assistance when one has no special obligation to do so. This feature of providing assistance is *not* due to there being no right to assistance, but is rather due to the way in which such rights may fall on no one in particular. In cases like that just mentioned, it is morally indifferent *who* among those in a position to do so provides the assistance, and so an individual does not necessarily fail in his duties if he waits to see whether anyone else provides the aid. To provide assistance which could equally well have been provided by others relieves the others of their obligation, and may amount to taking action *before* it is morally necessary. The rescuer relieves other potential rescuers of their burden and does so when he did not have to, and *that* is what is optional and supererogatory about providing aid in such circumstances.

There is even a place for praise and reward in cases in which there are no options with regard to who provides the assistance. Suppose someone is in need of assistance to prevent loss of life, and only one person is in a position to provide the aid. There is, say, only one person on the beach and aware of the drowning man's need for assistance. In such a case, the duty to provide assistance falls on that person even if it is entirely accidental that it is *he* who happens to be in that position. He experiences the drowning man's right to life as a demand on him in a way that others do not, even though there is otherwise no morally relevant difference between him and the others on whom the obligation does not fall. In the case of a negative right to life, the right is experienced as a restraint only by someone who contemplates doing something not allowed to others; a positive right to life, however, is experienced as a restraint also by someone like the lone rescuer on the beach even though if he were to fail to respect the right he would only be doing something allowed to others, viz, not providing aid. Not to respect a right to assistance in this circumstance is to act (in other respects) in the same way as everyone else, and to respect it is to accept burdens not imposed on everyone else even though the one on whom the burden falls is no more or less deserving than the others on whom it does not fall. There is a differential burden without differential merit. Resentment at having to accept such burdens is thus easily understandable, since it seems unfair that the one person should have to accept greater burdens for reasons having nothing to do with his own merit. This may explain the appropriateness of rewarding those who provide assistance: the rewards help to compensate them for the undeserved burden which has fallen on them. Rewards for assistance thus have a plausible rationale even if providing assistance is sometimes morally required.

Concerns about liberty, about praise, reward and supererogation, and

about justifying unacceptable kinds of killing thus do not pose serious difficulties for the idea of positive rights as such, provided that the conception
of positive rights presupposed by the foregoing remarks is workable. That
is, these concerns are not serious if it is possible to conceive positive rights
in a coherent way that does not impose excessive demands. But one of the
further worries about rights to assistance is just that of whether it is possible
to explicate satisfactorily the requirements imposed by such rights. Even
apart from the aforementioned concerns, there remains the skeptic's objection that there is no way to systematize our views on positive rights without
either falling into inconsistency or justifying too much or too little. I turn
next to some considerations which may help to meet the skeptic's challenge.

5.4. POSITIVE RIGHTS AND INDIVIDUAL ACTION

Just how much sacrifice may an individual be required to make under the
conception of positive rights proposed herein? To answer this question we
need some conception of what the various levels of sacrifice are. I shall
distinguish three levels of sacrifice which represent perhaps the most important major divisions along these lines. The differences between these levels
will not always be clear-cut, nor will the proposed characterization of them
always be sufficient to resolve the question of to which level a particular
sacrifice belongs. There are, however, clear cases of each type of sacrifice,
and I shall be mainly concerned with these.

In general, something may be considered a sacrifice for an individual
just when that individual has had the thing or could have had the thing,
wanted to have it, but gave it up or had it taken away for the sake of something considered more important. The main divisions in levels of sacrifice
are these. The most serious kinds of sacrifice are those which involve loss
of things necessary to the living of many or all kinds of lives. The importance
of these things is not dependent on someone's having chosen some relatively
specific life plan. Sacrifice of this sort may be called *major sacrifice*. Loss
of life itself is, of course, the clearest example of major sacrifice, but also
included here would be loss of such things as an arm or one's eyesight.
Having two arms is not necessary for every kind of life imaginable, but is
normally available to nearly everyone and is important for most kinds of
lives.

A second level of sacrifice is that of *moderate sacrifice*. This may be
defined as sacrifice of something which is important to the particular aims
and desires of an individual, but which is not vital to general functioning

as a person. Thus, loss of the land necessary to being a farmer, or of the musical instruments necessary to being a musician, would be moderate sacrifices for those individuals. Loss of money in amounts of, say, one thousand dollars would be a moderate sacrifice for most persons.

The third level is that of *trivial sacrifice*. Trivial sacrifice is the loss of something that is wanted by the person who loses it, but which is not important enough to that person's life to count as moderate or major sacrifice. Loss of a few dollars (say, five) or of a few moments of one's time would be examples of trivial sacrifice.

To determine how much sacrifice may be morally required of a person we must consider how the principle of respect for persons applies to the various levels. Our earlier discussion indicates that trivial sacrifice may be required, so let us here consider moderate sacrifice. We do require persons to make moderate sacrifices in order to avoid killing others. We are not justified in killing our employers merely because they plan to fire us, or in killing our children merely because they cost us money. The situation with regard to preventing death is, I shall argue, similar. Taken in isolation, a case in which one is required to make a moderate sacrifice to prevent another's death is no different from a case of enduring a moderate sacrifice in order to avoid killing. The reason is that if one fails to prevent a death because preventing the death would involve a moderate sacrifice, then one takes the lost goods as more important than the very life of another person. But the moral postulate operative here attributes to persons supreme importance. Thus to fail to prevent death when that would involve only moderate sacrifice is to fail to act in the way required by recognition of the moral status of persons; it is to place a higher value on the satisfaction of one's own wants than on others' lives.

Finally, then, may major sacrifice be required? I have indicated above that the principle of respect for persons does not allow that one person be sacrificed for the sake of another, but the defense of that needs more than the intuitive foundation provided so far. When Mary, for instance, refuses to give up her life to save Tom, why do we say that she has refused to sacrifice her own life rather than that she has sacrificed Tom's to preserve her own? Why does the life of the potential rescuer always seem to count more than the life of the one who needs to be rescued?

The basis for the view that a persons is not morally required to give up his or her own life to save another may be seen if we consider how the principle of respect for persons applies to that situation. Mary may rescue Tom only at the cost of her own life; why is she not required to do it?

Recall that the reason why a person may be required to make a less-than-major sacrifice to save another's life is that the failure to do so is tantamount to placing greater value on the person's own loss than on the other's life, and that such valuing is contrary to the principle that what is of greatest moral importance is that persons live lives of their own choosing. This case for required sacrifice cannot be made when the sacrifice is major. If Mary refuses to give up her own life for Tom's, she has not failed to recognize the supreme importance of persons because she has not placed something of less importance above the life of a person. Her own life is of equal moral importance, and so her refusal to sacrifice it is not in violation of the principle of respect for persons. She may make the sacrifice, but she is not required to do so. Further, since Mary is not required to make the sacrifice herself, third parties are not justified in forcing her to do so.

Since the viewpoint advanced here says that one may be required to make a moderate or lesser sacrifice for the sake of others' lives, it seems to involve a rather stringent morality. However, there are some considerations not yet fully explored which alter the picture significantly for many kinds of situations. One situation which illustrates some of the problems that may arise is that in which one is asked to contribute to, say, a charity designed to aid the needy. Contribution of even fairly large sums of money would often be no more than a moderate sacrifice, so if needed to save lives, such sacrifices could be required. Given enough need, this apparently leads to the result that all spending for luxuries may be wrong.

One way to attack this consequence is to consider the implications of requiring such assistance in all similar cases. If there are many similarly situated needy persons, then each would seem to have an equal claim to being aided by a benefactor, say, Jones. Now while assisting some of these persons would not be a major sacrifice for Jones, assisting all of them very well could be. Given enough needy persons, Jones could be required to devote his entire life and everything he has to their assistance. Even though individually none of the needy would require more than moderate sacrifice, aiding all the similarly situated would be a major sacrifice. Since aiding all would be a major sacrifice, the present view does not require such aid. However, the view may be taken that because responding to all similar cases of need would involve a major sacrifice, one is not required to respond to any such cases, since similar cases should be treated similarly.[4] This view is not persuasive because it does not follow from the fact that responding to all similar cases of need would require a major sacrifice that one is required to respond to no such cases. An alternative view is that one is required to respond to such cases up to the point at which further response would involve major sacrifice. If, for instance, it costs $1000 to provide aid to each person and amounts greater than $10 000 involve major sacrifice, then one is required to aid ten persons even if there are a thousand who need similar help. Barring special relationships, it is morally indifferent which ten one helps.

This alternative is the preferable way of handling cases in which providing assistance to all who need it would involve too great a sacrifice. The reason in favor of providing aid up to the point at which doing so involves too great a cost is the same as that where there is no question of significant sacrifice. That is, aid is required because it is necessary to the maintenance of persons and can be provided at no cost in terms of persons' functioning as persons. The only thing that sets the cases where many are in need apart from others is the principle that similar cases should be treated similarly. However, to require aid only to the point at which the cost becomes too great is not to violate this principle, for the very fact that the cost becomes so significant is a satisfactory reason for setting off further cases as different in a morally relevant way. Once the major cost point is reached, further cases are distinguished on the ground that providing aid would be a major sacrifice for the potential benefactor. There is no reason why that should not count as a relevant factor − if cost to the potential benefactor counts in distinguishing a case of saving a drowning man by throwing out a life preserver from a case of saving one by risking one's life in treacherous waters, then it should be relevant here, too. Thus, the view taken here is that one is required to provide aid up to the point at which assistance involves major cost, even if there are more cases of otherwise similar needy persons than can be assisted without major cost.

Since the principle that similar cases should be treated in similar ways fails to reduce significantly the extent to which an individual may be required to provide assistance, the approach being developed here still seems quite demanding. However, the application of the view to particular kinds of cases is not as unambiguous as it may seem, for numerous contingencies may affect apparently similar cases. For instance, in light of the foregoing, is one required to give money, say $10, to a charity the purpose of which is to save the lives of starving persons in famine-ridden areas? The apparent answer is that one *is* required to provide this aid, assuming that the $10 makes no major difference in one's own life. But this may not be the correct answer for many cases in which one is confronted with similar requests for donations. The case needs to be described in greater detail. The request for a donation has been made, let us suppose, of Jones. Jones has already given $1000 this year toward the assistance of others; moreover, for persons in Jones' circumstances $1000 per year marks the point beyond which monetary sacrifices become major interferences (e.g., Jones would not be able to feed his family if he gave more). To require Jones to contribute another $10 would be to require him to contribute a total of $1010, a major sacrifice; thus, Jones is not required to contribute the $10.

It may be objected that this example is unrealistically precise in its assumptions concerning the possibility of specifying the point at which a sacrifice becomes too great. Is it really plausible to suppose that $1010 could be a major sacrifice when $1000 is not? Whatever point is chosen as the limit, it is likely that some small amount could be added to it without making any difference plausibly regarded as significant. The answer to this objection, of course, is that we are dealing with a necessarily vague concept and we thus must draw some arbitrary lines just as we must in any case in which the question of whether a vague concept applies, is to determine an all-or-nothing outcome. Either Jones must contribute further or not, depending on whether the total contribution is a major interference. Any arbitrarily chosen line is acceptable provided that it is consistent with the clear meaning and application of the concept.

Consider next Smith's case. Like Jones, Smith is confronted with a request to contribute $10 toward the saving of lives. Unlike Jones, he has made no recent contribution to others' assistance, so he is not exempt from the requirement on the ground that exempts Jones. But consider the uncertainties Smith faces. Are the potential recipients of his donation truly in need of assistance? Perhaps the situation has been made to appear worse than it really is. Perhaps Smith has heard nothing of the situation in question before and must rely solely on the description of the person collecting dnoations. Further, even if the situation of the potential recipients of the donation is difficult, is it one they could readily eliminate on their own without assistance? One is not required to provide for others if they may easily provide for themselves, so this uncertainty will also leave Smith in doubt about whether he is required to provide aid.

Further difficulties arise when we consider the question of whether the requested donation will actually help those in need. There will of course be administrative costs involved in collecting and distributing donations; how much of a $10 contribution will actually be spent on those who need help? Will the amount that reaches them be enough to do any good? Perhaps it will be so small that it will not actually save anyone; the sort of difficulty being suffered might be one that can be alleviated only by contributions totaling to some minimum amount. Perhaps the difficulty is one that will not be alleviated by *money* in any amount.

These kinds of uncertainty and more can be seen to be present in many of the actual situations in which assistance may be needed. One sees a child wandering by a highway — but perhaps its mother is nearby and merely out of sight. Three men appear to be beating another — but perhaps they are plain-clothes policement making an arrest.[5] A woman cries desperately for help — but perhaps it is really only an overly dramatic and public family quarrel for which no assistance is needed or welcome.[6] To know whether assistance is needed one must know facts about the abilities, intentions and circumstances of others that are often not readily ascertainable. This is in sharp contrast to what is required to respect others' rights against being positively harmed. Normally one need know nothing more than one's own intentions and some obvious empirical facts to know whether one is doing what is called for by such rights. With rights to assistance, one may rarely know with certainty whether one is doing what respect for those rights requires.

Other cases also involve uncertainty with respect to the cost involved in providing aid. When asked to give $10, one is at least clear about what sacrifice one is being asked to make, but if, say, the case involves swimming out to save someone drowing, it may be very uncertain how much cost will be involved — perhaps it will be no more than some wet clothes and a few lost minutes, but potential rescuers sometimes drown. Furthermore, one sometimes may be uncertain about just what kind of aid is needed. Someone ignorant of first aid may be willing to help but not know what procedure is needed in a given case.

Another difficulty can be seen in cases such as that in which one is asked to contribute to the support of some specific individual who will not have enough to eat without assistance. It may be that an insignificant (to the benefactor) contribution of $10 might be enough to support such a person for a few days, but suppose that the person is permanently unable to support himself. What he really needs is support probably for the rest of his life, but providing that might well be too great a sacrifice for someone who could easily make the $10 contribution. In that circumstance, is one required to provide the temporary aid, even though it would only postpone rather than eliminate the real problem? Here aid would be required only if it would postpone severe and irreversible harm which is imminent. In that event, at least the immediate problem would be curable through the insignificant

sacrifice one might be able to make. However, one would not be required
to contribute to the less immediate problem when that would make no real
difference to that problem. In that case, one would be required to contribute
only if enough others contributed so that it became possible to eliminate
the problem without requiring anyone to make a major sacrifice. Since one
might be uncertain whether others will make the requisite sacrifice, it may
be unclear whether any sacrifice is required.

The problem immediately at hand is that of the effect of all these uncertainties on the moral assessment of actual situations in which aid may be
needed. Uncertainties can exist with respect to whether aid is needed, what
kind of aid is needed, how much cost would be involved for the helper, and
whether the helper(s) will be able to provide the aid needed. When these
uncertainties exist, is one required to provide assistance? Obviously an agent
faced with a decision about whether his or her assistance is required in a
given situation should make a sincere effort to determine the true nature
of the situation and can be expected to do no better than to act on his or
her own best judgment, but given that in some cases a person's best judgment
may be that it is uncertain whether assistance is required, the problem is not
resolved with this. What must be considered is whether the principle which
accords each person special moral importance requires assistance when
uncertainty exists.

Where uncertainty exists, action or omission involves risk. If it is uncertain
what the effects of a course of action will be and among the possible effects
is something undesirable, then performance of the action involves risk.
Similarly, if it is uncertain whether others need assistance to avoid some
harmful result, then failure to assist involves risk. It is clear that the total
avoidance of all risk is not required. If that were required, much of modern
life would be unacceptable, for much of it involves or depends on activity
which increases the risk of harm to persons. The use of automobiles and
aircraft, the building of dams, the production of many kinds of goods, and
much more all involve the presence of risks that otherwise would be absent.
Taking small risks, however, is not unacceptable since taking small risks
with something is not inconsistent with holding it to be of the greatest
importance. We find nothing odd, for instance, in a person's claiming that
he holds his own life to be most important to him while being willing to take
small risks with his life – say, by driving automobiles or riding in airplanes
– for the sake of ends he takes to be less important.

In contrast, one would be required to avoid actions or omissions involving
serious risk to others. Such activities would be consistent with viewing

persons as supremely important only if it were acceptable to take serious risks with that which one considers so important. But since performance of a highly risky activity is tantamount to preferring the activity or its ends to that which is risked, performance of such actions is not consistent with holding persons to be of greatest importance.

The failure to assist someone may involve risk of harmful consequences that could be prevented through assistance. Since small risks are permissible and serious risks are not, failure to assist is permissible when there is only a small chance that assistance is needed, and impermissible when it is highly probable that assistance is vitally needed. What, then, must we say of our everyday failures to assist others? As we go about the activities we have chosen, we constantly take the risk that our omissions will allow serious harm to occur. Consider, however, what it would take to avoid this kind of risk. To be certain that we are not failing to provide assistance that we could provide, we would have to devote ourselves primarily to determining when and where assistance is needed; the effort required to be certain that our omissions are innocent would be so great as to leave no room for living a life of one's own choosing. Such a stringent requirement thus would not be imposed by a principle requiring that each person be allowed to live a life of his or her own choosing.

A wide variety of cases could arise in which a person has a special opportunity to provide assistance. Consideration of one of these will allow some further implications to be brought out. One type of case is exemplified in the following. Jones drives his car past two men standing on a corner. One of the men is behaving in a threatening manner toward the other. No weapons are visible, but the apparent aggressor looks capable of inflicting severe injury on the other. It could be no more than an animated argument, but it is possible that the apparent aggressor intends to injure or even kill the second man. Is Jones required to stop to call the police or to inquire further into the nature of the situation? There is some reason to think that the second man needs assistance, but on the basis of what Jones knows of the case this is something less than likely. It is at least as likely that the man is not in serious danger.

The case for required assistance in a situation such as this is weak. Even though there is some reason to suspect that the man may need help, since it is just as likely that he does not, assistance is not required. The failure to provide aid here does not, in itself, reflect a disregard for the moral importance of persons since there is very good chance that no one is in danger. A case for required assistance in this situation could be made out only with the assumption that a very conservative attitude toward risk is required. That is, avoiding the risk would be required only if holding something to be of supreme importance precludes taking risks with it for the sake of other desired aims, albeit less important ones. Where the probability of losing the more valued thing is not high, there is no reason to think that risking it for the sake of something less valued is inconsistent or otherwise irrational. It is not uncommon for people to risk their lives for the sake of ends they do not take to be more important than life. Not everyone in a dangerous occuption, for instance, believes that the attractions of a risky life are more important than life itself. Yet there is no apparent reason to deem their willingness to take risks inconsistent with their professed ordering of values.[7] Thus, where there is less than a substantial probability that aid is actually needed, it is not *required* that aid be provided.

A second consideration which significantly reduces the demands that rights to assistance make on individuals acting as individuals is that of fairness in the distribution of the burdens of providing assistance. Suppose that we have a case in which vital assistance may be provided to a group of needy persons by expenditures totaling one million dollars. Providing vital health care to those who would not otherwise have it might be an example of the kind of assistance relevant here. On whom should the burden of providing this assistance fall? The foregoing considerations indicate that it should be provided by those in a position to assist. If this is a group of one thousand equally well-off persons and none of them has any special obligation to provide the aid, then a fair distribution of the burden would obviously call for each of the thousand persons to contribute one thousand dollars. Each person would be required to provide the thousand dollars because the failure to do so would be a failure to act with the requisite respect for the importance of those persons whose lives are at stake. The thousand dollars represents only a moderate sacrifice for the persons involved, and thus it is not a sacrifice great enough to excuse the failure to provide aid.

The general implication of this is that an individual is required to contribute a fair share of the assistance called for by respect for the moral status of persons. While this means that one may be called on to make a moderate sacrifice for the sake of others, it also potentially limits the amount of sacrifice one may be required to make. For if one is required to contribute *only* one's fair share and no more, then the amount one is required to contribute at a given time depends upon what amount constitutes a fair share of the burden and upon how much of that share one has already contributed, not upon whether the needs of others are fully satisfied or upon whether satisfying them would require a major sacrifice. If one is required to assume only a fair share of the burden, then one is not required to make further sacrifices once one has fulfilled one's share. If this is correct, those who have contributed a fair share are not prohibited from spending their money as they please even if further contributions on their part would provide additional vital assistance. Luxurious living need not be a violation of rights to assistance even in a world in which not everyone's needs are satisfied, provided that individuals are required to contribute only fair shares.

The major reason for doubt about this interpretation of the requirement of respect for persons is that there is a strong *prima facie* case for the more stringent interpretation. Suppose that there are a thousand persons in a position to contribute vital health care for another group of persons who cannot provide it for themselves, and that this care may be obtained for one million dollars. A fair share for each of the benefactors is one thousand dollars. If each of the thousand contributes his fair share, all is well. However, suppose that only fifty percent of the potential benefactors actually contribute the thousand dollars they are morally required to contribute. Then it will be impossible to provide vital assistance to some of those who need it. Are those who have given their fair share required to make additional contributions? From one perspective, it would seem that the case for required additional assistance in this circumstance is as strong as in the initial instance, since (we may suppose) those who have given their fair shares could give more without making a major sacrifice. Apparently, to fail to give more would be to fail to treat the personhood of others as of greater importance than that which would be sacrificed in the giving of additional aid.

There are countervailing considerations which may alter the status of the failure to provide aid in the special circumstances of this situation. If aid were required beyond one's fair share, those who contributed their fair shares would be required to make additional contributions because the other potential benefactors failed to make the sacrifice which they are morally required to make. In that case, those who choose to act wrongly by failing to contribute are able to impose additional requirements on others *merely by choosing to do so*. The wrongdoer seems to be given, in effect, control over the actions of others, since he or she is in a position to determine by choice what others are required to do. This consequence is questionable on respect-for-persons grounds. This seems to allow a wrongdoer control over the lives of others that could not be permitted by the respect-for-persons viewpoint.

One conclusion which might be promised in light of these considerations is that persons have no duty to act when the need for action exists only because of someone else's failure to do what is required. It is unlikely, however, that such a conclusion could be reconciled with considered judgements about many cases. Take the Kitty Genovese case, in which many persons heard the cries for help of a woman being attacked, but failed to do even so much as call the police for help. This sort of case has stimulated some public demand for legal requirements to aid others, but if the wrongful actions of others cannot create moral requirements for persons, such laws would not be appropriate. But required aid does seem appropriate here and in other cases. The fact that someone else has failed to make the minimal effort necessary to save, say, a drowning child does not seem to entail that the next person has no duty to act. The argument that the failure to aid is a failure to recognize the supreme importance of persons is thus not inappropriate even when the need is created by the wrongful acts of others. Further, there are other cases in which there is no problem about the fact that others' choices create duties for a person. The fact that other persons have chosen to be on the highway does generate a duty not to drive in certain ways.

The implications of the fair share factor are thus somewhat complex. The fact that someone has contributed a fair share toward providing vital assistance does not necessarily mean that further contributions are not required; they may be required because others fail to contribute their fair shares. However, given that an individual has contributed a fair share, he or she may respond to the wrongful omissions of others in more than one way. Rather than simply accepting the demand that one contribute further, one could react to the situation by attempting to get those who have failed to do their part to do so. The fair shares factor marks the point beyond which one is required to contribute further only if others fail to do what is required of them; the use of force in getting others to do their part may be acceptable.

The concern about positive rights which generated this discussion was, again, that recognition of positive rights may impose such excessive demands as to make them unreasonable. It may now be shown that this is not the case. The fair shares factor and the uncertainty factor combine to prevent drawing the conclusion that relatively comfortable individuals must, *as individuals*, abandon their advantages to provide aid to others. They are required to contribute their fair shares, and that may involve giving up some advantages, but given that an individual has contributed his or her fair share, there are several reasons why further actions may not be required in typical circumstances. First, insofar as there are means available to force individuals to contribute further (e.g., through the state), those who have not contributed their fair shares are obviously the ones who should be made to do so, not the individual we are concerned with. Second, if such coercion is unsuccessful or is not attempted, any duty which then falls on those who have contributed fair shares depends upon whether there is anything that can be done without accepting a major sacrifice. The main options here are either to find a way to get those who are failing to do what is required to do it, or to do it oneself. In either case, circumstances may not call for further required aid. First, it may not be possible for the individual to do anything to provide needed aid in view of others' refusal to cooperate. It may be something that one person, or those who are willing to act, simply cannot do. Second, it may be something which would require too great a sacrifice for those who have contributed their fair shares. If the sacrifice becomes major, it is not required. Third, it may be that there is nothing the individuals may do which is likely enough to make a difference that it could be required. One is not required to act merely because it is possible that aid might be obtained; omissions involving some risk are permitted. Thus, individuals often may not be required to contribute more than a fair share because of these factors. I hasten to add, however, that this does not mean that there is not good reason to make optional contributions, nor does it mean that there is no duty to provide aid through collective action.

5.5. POSITIVE RIGHTS, THE STATE, AND COLLECTIVE ACTION

The sphere in which positive rights have their most important consequences is that of the evaluation of the actions of groups of persons, especially when they act through the state. As the above discussion of fair shares suggests, collective action makes it possible to provide assistance which no individual would be required to provide. The expense and effort necessary to provide health care for all of those who could not otherwise have it, for instance, could easily become a major sacrifice for an individual, and thus would not be required. Acting collectively, however, a group of persons could provide extensive aid without unduly burdening any individual. Even very trivial sacrifices, such as the contribution of a dollar or two, could make possible the provision of large amounts of aid, given enough contributors. Since even moderate sacrifices may be required of an individual, however, the amount of aid that could be provided by a group of persons, none of whom makes a greater sacrifice than may be required, is very great indeed.

Providing assistance collectively, unlike providing it individually, often requires organization. The most likely form of collective assistance is monetary, and that may require management if it is to achieve its purpose. A check for a thousand dollars sent to a starving family in a famine-ridden area might be utterly useless, as it would be if there were no food in the area to buy with it. The requisite organizations might take any number of forms, but of principal importance would be government or the state. No other organization purports to represent more than a subset of the persons in a given area, and so no other organization is in a position to act as agent for all of those who may be required to provide vital assistance. Even when no other appropriate organization through which to provide vital aid is available, the existence of government makes providing assistance possible, and therefore morally necessary. The possibility of collective action through government means that there is likely to be no excuse for the failure of advantaged groups to assist groups whose ability to function as persons is threatened. Indeed, it may even be that it would be morally necessary to establish a state, if none existed; the only barrier to this might be the difficulty of doing so.

The existence of organized groups is of further significance in that when the burden of responding to rights to assistance falls on organized groups it is less likely that some of the uncertainties which weaken the requirement to provide assistance as it applies to individuals will be present in a similar form. It will often be possible for a group, acting through its agents, to conduct investigations which will remove the uncertainties an individual could not be expected to be able to eliminate. Groups may have the resources to determine whether aid is really needed, what kind is needed, and how much is needed. They are also likely to be able to be certain that the aid will reach its intended recipients. Further, by ensuring that everyone able to contribute does contribute, a collective entity such as a state can guarantee that enough funds will be collected to actually provide the needed aid. So if the needs in question will be satisfied only if some minimum threshold is surpassed, the state may be able to ensure that it is surpassed; an individual asked to make a voluntary contribution in the same circumstances would be unlikely to be able to determine whether the threshold will be reached. An individual also is much less likely to be able to determine accurately what is a fair share of the burden necessary to provide required assistance, while government may be able to conduct the studies which would answer that question with some reliability. Finally, it is much less likely that assistance provided collectively will involve risk of major sacrifice. Individual action, such as attempting to save someone drowning, may not be required because the only available method of rescue involves risk of loss of life for the rescuer. Collective action, such as purchasing needed aid through monies collectively provided, will seldom involve this kind of risk. Even if there is uncertainty about how much money will be required to provide assistance, there is in general no likelihood that it will be impossible to prevent the sacrifice involved from becoming major. Collective assistance is much more likely to be morally required because the circumstances which render individual assistance optional are much less likely to be present.

In this we have a basis for a welfare principle. The *welfare principle* may be formulated in the following way:

> It is not a violation of the principle of respect for persons to use legal coercion to require persons to aid others, provided that what is required is (or is quite likely to be) vital to the personal functioning (functioning as persons) of those aided, and provided that the burden of bringing aid is fairly distributed and does not impose a major sacrifice on anyone.

The basis of this principle, of course, is the requirement that aid be brought to those whose ability to function as persons is threatened; the limitation to less-than-major sacrifice is based on the denial that some persons may be sacrificed for the benefit of others. The fair shares limitation requires some further explanation, however, because, as we saw in the preceding section, an individual's duties to aid others may exceed the fair shares limitation in some circumstances. The explanation is that since the welfare principle deals with the possibility of using force to bring aid, it should call for the use of force against those who have failed to contribute a fair share rather than those who have. Those who have contributed are not necessarily required to contribute further. They are required (at most) *either* to contribute further *or* to find a way to get those who have not, to do so. The action of the state against those who have not may be seen as an attempt to do the latter. Those who have contributed thus have a claim to being left alone, that those who have not, do not have.

That the welfare principle claims that it may be justifiable to use *force* to require persons to aid others may be seen by some as too strong. Even if it is admitted that aid is sometimes morally required, it may be claimed that the use of force to secure compliance with this requirement is unacceptable. The response to this position is twofold. First, since the arguments which show that providing aid is sometimes required are based on the same principle and consideration as the arguments which show that not harming persons is morally required, there is no reason to think that violations of the requirements should be handled differently. Second, it is not at all clear that considered judgments support the view that force or coercion may not be used to require persons to aid others. I shall describe one example which seems to provide strong support for the contrary view.

Take the case of a man — let us call him Andrew — who has recently been in an accident. Andrew's injuries were such that he was put in a cast which leaves only one arm free; he is unable to use his legs or his left arm, and he is unable to move from his bed. Because of Andrew's lack of mobility, two business acquaintances of his have agreed to meet him at his bedside to carry out a business transaction. When the two men arrive in Andrew's bedroom, one of them removes his coat and hangs it in the closet across the room from Andrew's bed. As they begin their discussion, the man who removed his coat suddenly gets a very distressed look on his face, starts to make a move toward the closet, but falls to the floor, gasping and clutching at his chest. Unable to get up, he weakly asks the other man to get his pills out of his jacket. This man, however, knows that he stands to gain a great deal financially if the stricken man dies; thinking that this is something he will be able to get away with, he refuses to help. Andrew knows that the stricken man has a heart condition and is likely to die without the pills. Now if Andrew has a gun under his pillow, would it be morally wrong for him to use his one good arm to pull out the gun and threaten the second man with it in order to save the life of the first? This would be force or coercion just as much as would be the your-money-or-your-life threat of the gunman on the street; yet I submit that in this circumstance it would be perfectly acceptable. In this example, then, we have a case of justifiable use of force to require someone to come to the aid of another.

The welfare principle is also subject to a charge of vagueness. It asserts that legal coercion may be used to bring aid vital to someone's functioning as a person, but the boundaries of what is essential to personhood have not been set. Now I am inclined to see this problem as calling for a theory of social justice, i.e., a theory defining what a just society must guarantee for all. This seems a task large enough to warrant independent treatment. The extent of the present discussion has been guided by the thought that it should show the legitimacy of the general class of legal requirements that persons contribute to the welfare of others. I have endeavored to do this by explaining how respect-for-persons ethics can require that persons sometimes come to the aid of those whose lives are endangered. This at least shows that some version of the welfare principle is part of the respect-for-persons approach.

The welfare principle is essential to the justification of many kinds of legislation. Its primary use will be in connection with various kinds of legislation designed to ensure that everyone attains the minimum level necessary to functioning as a person. This would be likely to include such things as assistance in buying food, paying for health care, obtaining basic educational opportunities, and so on. It is also an important principle for defending the taxation used to support governmental programs, not only because the funds so collected could be used to buy such things as those just mentioned, but also because taxes support things like police protection. In this regard, paying taxes may be seen as a form of assistance in that doing so helps to provide others with this protection.[8]

CHAPTER SIX

THE PRINCIPLE OF COMMUNITY

6.1. INTRODUCTION

There remains an important sphere of possible legal interference not clearly affected by the foregoing principles. When the law intervenes to prevent harm to oneself or others, the intervention is justified, if at all, because it serves to protect a *person* in a legitimate way. However, sometimes actions pose no threat to persons sufficient to warrant intervention. What persons do with *things* other than persons is an example. May coercive law ever be used to interfere with what persons do with things (where there is no direct threat to persons)?

One way of answering this question can be ruled out quickly. Respect-for-persons ethics cannot permit interference with what persons do with things for the sake of the things themselves. This is because the primary commitment is to persons' having control over their own lives; the only interferences consistent with this commitment are those grounded in concern for this control. To interfere with persons for the sake of protecting non-persons would be to abandon this commitment. Thus, things can be protected from persons only when the protection is derivative from the moral importance of persons. As we saw in Section 3.2, this condition can be satisfied when a thing belongs to a person and thus lies within his or her personal sphere. The question now is whether there are other cases in which interference with what persons do with things may be justified. Since the law may not interfere for the sake of things themselves, we must look to whether respect for persons' control over their own lives can be understood to include control over things beyond individual belongings. The question of what the law may be used to do in this area depends upon who should be in control.

6.2. LAISSEZ-FAIRE VERSUS COLLECTIVE CONTROL

Consider, as an example, the decision concerning how a lake shared by all members of a community shall be used.[1] Ten families live on the lake, and traditionally they have all used the lack for swimming, fishing, and as a place to dump raw sewage. However, use of the lake for sewage now

76

threatens to make it unfit for swimming and fishing; it is no longer possible to use the lake for all three purposes. If septic tanks are installed soon, the lake can be saved; it could, however, be used for sewage disposal without causing any disadvantage beyond the loss of a site for swimming and fishing. Now, who should decide to which use this lake shall be put? The decision is not obviously assigned to any individual, and this leaves open the question of how the fate of the lake should be determined.

Two alternatives require consideration. One is to allow the fate of the lake to be determined by the results of the individual decisions of the various persons involved. On this approach no decision is made to the effect that *this* is how the lake shall be used; instead, each family decides how it shall use the lake, and what happens to the lake depends upon these various individual choices. If each family decided that it shall stop using the lake for sewage disposal, then it will remain available for swimming and fishing, but if enough families decide to continue discharging sewage into the lake so that it does become unfit for the other uses, then the lake's fate is determined regardless of what the remaining families decide to do. This laissez-faire approach is traditionally the one favored by the champions of individual liberty, and it clearly has some obvious merits from that viewpoint. No one seems to be forced into doing anything or into refraining from anything. Those who use the lake for swimming and fishing do not thereby prevent others from using it for sewage, nor do those who use it for sewage thereby prevent others from using it for swimming. Would-be swimmers could still swim in the polluted lake, and if they choose not to, it is not because of coercion, but because of a change in the character of the lake not easily condemned as coercive. Much the same could be said about fishing. However, there is something very troubling about this as a way of securing for individuals control over their own lives. Although those who wish to use the lake for swimming and fishing are not coerced into accepting the other use, their preferences under the circumstances have no real chance of prevailing, and carry virtually no weight in determining the outcome.

The other alternative in determining how the lake shall be used is collective decision.[2] The ten families could decide to use the lake in the way they most prefer, and those who prefer the other use would have to accept the collective decision. On this approach everyone would express a preference concerning how the lake should be used rather than simply making a choice about how he or she shall use it. An advantage of this method is that it guarantees that more people will be satisfied with the results than with the laissez-faire approach, since the latter allows the possibility that the wishes of the majority might be thwarted by a minority. That would be the case if, say, only one family chooses to continue dumping sewage into the lake and that is sufficient to make it unfit for the other uses. Unfortunately, this advantage is not a sufficient justification for the collective decision approach, since it is subject to the objection that this is to sacrifice the liberty of the minority to satisfy the preferences of a majority. After all, enforcing the collective decision to save the lake for swimming and fishing may involve forcing the dissenting family not to dump sewage in the lake. What is involved here is much more clearly coercion than is that one family's pollution of the lake resulting in its not being used for swimming and fishing. So collective decision may involve apparently objectionable coercion.

Can it be justifiable to use legal coercion to enforce a collective decision such as that involved in the lake example? In asking this question, it is important to distinguish it from various other questions which may be asked about such cases. For instance, there are questions relating to the matter of what is the *efficient* outcome for lake-type cases, and of how that outcome can be achieved. From this perspective, an outcome is efficient in the event that there is no change in the outcome which would make someone better off without making someone else worse off. In this sense, an efficient outcome in the lake case might be achieved by allowing the families who want the lake saved for fishing and swimming to bargain with the other family, offering the latter something else it values in exchange for its restraint on use of the lake for sewage disposal. Such bargains might involve an exchange of private property or of other things or services valued by the persons involved.

Such possibilities are essentially variants of the laissez-faire approach. They share the characteristic that they provide for no authoritative decision with regard to the fate of the lake; instead, that outcome is left to be determined by the cumulative effect of the various individual decisions made by the persons involved. The result achieved by a laissez-faire approach may be the same as that favored by collective decision, but there can be no guarantee that this will be the case. The families who wish to save the lake for swimming and fishing, for instance, may not be able to offer the remaining family anything the latter values enough to secure its restraint. Thus, there remains a choice to be made between laissez-faire approaches and collective decision. In the terms of the present theory, the question here is a moral one, not one of efficiency. We have seen that there is some reason to think that interference with individual decisions for the sake of securing an outcome favored by a majority is morally unacceptable. Are these reasons decisive? Must a society acquiesce in the effects of laissez-faire, or may it use legal coercion to bring about specific results which it prefers?

In the present context, the problem is one of whether the principle of respect for persons permits enforcement of collective decisions in such cases as these. That principle demands that priority be given to everyone's having control over his or her own life; thus, the question becomes one of whether collective control or laissez-faire better respects this demand. Some advantages of laissez-faire have been noted; let us look more closely at its disadvantages. Consider further the case in which nine families prefer that the lake be used for fishing and swimming, while one prefers to dump sewage into it. Where one family's sewage is sufficient to make the lake unfit for the other uses, any one family's choosing to use the lake for sewage disposal has the effect of determining that the lake will be used for that purpose rather than the others. The question of whose preferences will be satisfied is answered through the relationship between the competing uses of the lake. The activities of swimming and fishing do not interfere with the dumping of sewage into the lake, but the latter does interfere with the former. Because of this relationship, the laissez-faire approach guarantees that anyone who prefers use of the lake for sewage disposal may have his or her way, while it makes it quite difficult for anyone who favors the other alternative to have what that person wants. Whether one may have things the way one wants them, depends on natural contingencies over which one has no control.

Another case is that in which the relationship between competing activities is more equal. Suppose, for instance, that some want to use the lake for disposal of waste chemicals, while others want to fill it in to obtain additional farm land. If the chemicals are such that their presence will be harmful to crops grown on the reclaimed land, we have a situation in which each use of the lake interferes with the other. Filling in the lake makes it impossible to use it for disposal of chemicals, and using it for chemical disposal makes it impossible to use as farmland. In this case, unlike the first, those who favor the competing uses seem to be on an equal footing under the laissez-faire approach. However, in this case which use is actually made of the lake is determined on a first-come, first-served basis; once the lake has been used in one of these ways, it cannot be used in the other. Thus, in this kind of case, the actual use of the lake is determined by the preferences of the person who happens to be first to use it, regardless of the reason why this person rather than another happens to be first on the scene.

I want to argue that these cases exemplify the way in which allowing outcomes to be determined in a laissez-faire manner can be undesirable from a respect-for-persons point of view. The difficulty lies in the differential control which can result from laissez-faire determinations of outcomes. Under laissez-faire, some people find themselves in control of situations and others find themselves subject to the control of those persons, and the question of who is in which position is determined by factors which are essentially accidental from a human point of view. Let us focus for a moment on the case of using the lake for sewage disposal versus using it for swimming and fishing. In one sense, there is complete equality between the ten families living on the lake, since (we may suppose) each has the same ability to influence the outcome. That is, any family may contribute to saving the lake by refraining from using it for sewage disposal, and any family may defeat the attempt to save the lake by continuing to use it for sewage disposal. Since there is in this respect an equality of influence, it may not be apparent why laissez-faire is open to the charge of allowing differential control. The explanation lies in a distinction between *influence* and *control*.

To influence something is, in one sense, to have an effect upon its condition or development. A runner in a race, for instance, can typically influence the results of the race – the order in which the runners finish – by the way in which she runs in the race. If she puts forth less than full effort, she can influence the final standings by finishing farther back than would have been possible. To influence something, however, is not yet to *control* it. Our runner does not control the results of the race simply because she can slow down and thereby finish lower in the final standings. Control requires not merely the ability to influence results, but the ability to influence them in such a way that one achieves the results one wants. A runner who wants to win a race but is not able to run as fast as the competition lacks an element of control over her standing in the race. A runner who can outrun the competition at will comes much closer to having full control over her finish. To have *full unilateral control* over a result is to be able to produce the result one wants regardless of what others do or want. Thus, a person's control may be diminished in either of two ways. One is by inability to use the influence one has to produce the result one wants. If I am captured by terrorists who give me a choice between two methods, one of which they will use to execute me, I lack an important element of control over my situation. I have influence, but I lack control because I am not able to use it to produce the result I want. Similarly, if I am driving down an icy highway and my car goes into a skid when I attempt to go around a curve, I have lost control of the car – despite the fact that what I do next (e.g., whether or not I turn the wheels in the direction of the skid) may influence what happens. The other way in which a person's control may be less than full unilateral control is by inability to produce a result without the cooperation of others. I lack, for instance, full unilateral control over whether I buy a house if my doing so depends upon whether someone else lends me money. A group of people may have full control — imagine the members of a club choosing a name for their club — where no individual has full control, but shares control with others in the group. Further, control over something does not seem to require that one be able to do just anything with the thing controlled. A baseball pitcher has control if he is able to make the ball do what he wants it to do, or if he is able to make it do what pitchers typically want baseballs to do. He does not lack control because he is not able to throw the ball at a speed of five thousand miles per hour. Finally, we should note that control is not simply a matter of getting what one wants. A child who gets everything he wants at Chirstmas does not necessarily control what goes under the tree on Christmas Eve; he may simply have generous — perhaps too generous — parents who fully understand his wants. To have control is to be able to *bring about* the results one wants.

Summarizing these observations concerning control, it seems that a person lacks control over a result if any of the following conditions obtain. First, a person lacks control if what he or she does has no effect on the result. Second, a person lacks full unilateral control if what he or she does cannot bring about the results desired, even if such action can have some effect on the result. Third, a person lacks full unilateral control if the result he or she desires can be brought about only with the cooperation of others.

Returning now to the case of the lake, we can see that while the various families have an equal ability to influence the outcome for the lake, they do not have equal control over the outcome. The families which want to save the lake are not able to effectively bring about the result they want; they cannot effectively use their influence to produce the outcome they prefer. They therefore lack control because of their limited ability to contribute to the result they want and because the contribution they can make will be effective only with the cooperation of others. Contrast their situation with that of the family which does not want to save the lake. This family has much greater control in that it can effectively produce the result it wants. It can do so simply by continuing to dump sewage into the lake; this does not require the cooperation of others and it is an action which can bring about the *desired* results effectively. Further, this family exerts a kind of control over the others as well, since they could have what they want but for the decisions of this one family. The dissenting family gets to decide whether the others get what they want, while the others cannot, under laissez-faire, exert a similar control over whether the dissenters have what they want. Thus there is a substantial difference between the amounts of control possessed by the various families in this situation.

Collective decision is an alternative which avoids this accidental conferral of differential control which can result from allowing outcomes to be determined in a laissez-faire manner. If each person has a vote and the outcome is determined by the results of the vote, then we have a procedure which confers equal influence on each person, but it is influence which is equally effective in bringing about either or any result. That is, each person's vote contributes to the result he or she wants to the same extent as anyone else's vote contributes to the result that that person wants. This is in sharp contrast to the situation under laissez-faire, where it is possible for one party's 'vote' to fully accomplish the result wanted while another party's 'vote' can only make a small contribution to the result that person prefers. Collective decision provides that everyone shall have equal influence and that the influence of each shall be equally effective in producing whatever result is desired.

The principle of respect for persons does not demand that outcomes be determined in a laissez-faire manner. A comparison between collective decision and laissez-faire from the respect-for-persons viewpoint favors collective decision. It does so because collective decision better reflects the respect-for-persons commitment to the importance of every person's having control over his or her life. Laissez-faire remains indifferent to the seriously unequal control which can arise in lake-type cases; it demands that the many families must acquiesce in the choices of the one which happens to find itself in the advantageous position. Collective decision, however, does perhaps all that can be done to confer some control on everyone and to prevent individuals from gaining control over the lives of others. Since the basic commitment is respect for everyone's control, the outcome determination procedure which confers some control on everyone must be preferred to one which allows some much greater control, including control of others, in circumstances when this is avoidable.

There are, of course, some aspects of collective control which make it less than fully attractive from the respect-for-persons viewpoint. Collective control does not eliminate the problem that for most decisions there will be some who do not get what they want, nor the perhaps more serious problem that there may be some who never get what they want with collective decision. It also does not completely equalize influence between persons, since some persons may be able to influence the votes of others more effectively. These problems, however, do not undermine the argument that collective decision may be used to overrule the results of laissez-faire.

The fact that some may be consistent losers under collective decision is presumably a more serious problem than that some will be losers in a particular case. The latter problem is part of what generates the need for a decision procedure and presumably is present in any conceivable procedure. The problem of the consistent loser, however, is a distinct problem. Someone who is always on the losing side of every vote seems to be no better off under collective decision than under laissez-faire. There are two responses to this problem. First, it does not undercut the *comparative* claim that collective decision is better than laissez-faire, since both ways of determining outcomes may leave some persons as consistent losers. Second, there is at least one respect in which the consistent loser *is* better off (i.e., treated more as he or she should be treated) under collective decision, viz, the loser is given as much control over the outcomes as any other individual person, and that may not be the case under laissez-faire. Further, there may be ways of setting up collective decision procedures which would reduce or eliminate this difficulty. For instance, perhaps it could be provided that minorities be granted full control over some decisions, perhaps to an extent proportional to their numbers. There is, after all, nothing in the argument for collective decision which requires that all collective decisions be made in the way favored by a simple majority. It must also be remembered that minorities are protected in many ways by the harm principle and the welfare principle, so less rides on this question than might be thought.

The fact that some persons are more persuasive or charismatic than others is also not a sufficient objection to the claim that collective decision better respects persons. For one thing, this is another objection which applies to both collective decision and laissez-faire. Those who are able to persuade others to do what they want them to will be at an advantage under any method of determining outcomes which allows people to attempt to influence each other, so this point provides no reason to favor laissez-faire over collective decision. Further, it is not clear that there is necessarily anything objectionable about the fact that some people consistently may be able to use their influence with others to get what they want through collective decision. Whether this is a problem depends upon the nature of their influence over other voters. If the influence is achieved by deception, then the votes of the others are encumbered, and of course in that event the decision procedure fails to allow persons to have the unencumbered control to which they are entitled. But this problem calls for caution with respect to the procedures which lead to the vote, and is not an objection to collective decision itself. If the influence is achieved by means which do not encumber people's choices, then it is unobjectionable, for the influential person gains his or her influence through the choices of others; they choose to confer it upon that person. This in sharp contrast to the situation under laissez-faire, in which a person may find herself in control over others because of an indefinite range of natural contingencies. The person who gets what she wants by winning others' unencumbered approval has done all that need be done to respect their control. The mark which distinguishes collective control from laissez-faire in this regard is that only under collective control does the influential person's influence operate through the choices of others who play as great a role in the final decision as that person.

Thus, persons are not required to acquiesce in the effects of laissez-faire in lake-type cases because the alternative of collective decision better respects the commitment to each person's having control over his or her own life. Laissez-faire allows some persons to gain control over aspects of the lives of others, while collective decision provides each person with as much control as anyone else. Winning under collective decision is a function of people's exercise of control over their own lives.

6.3. THE SCOPE OF COLLECTIVE CONTROL

Completing the argument for collective control requires identification of the kinds of cases to which it applies. Which cases are 'lake-type' cases? This question is vital, since the argument for collective control is valid only for certain situations and not in general.

As an aid in identification of cases for which collective control is valid, I shall make use of the expression 'the common'. By 'the common' shall be meant something related to, but not identical with, the standard meaning of that expression. Ordinarily, the term denotes land which all have the right to use. As I shall use it, its denotation is not restricted to land, nor does it refer necessarily to use; it also does not designate things identified through conventional agreement. That is, while the term ordinarily refers to property designated for use by all through conventional agreement, on my use something's being part of the common does not depend on convention. This is because, as noted earlier, we are concerned to determine what may be said about control of things in the world independently of conventional arrangements. What 'the common' shall denote is everything other than persons themselves. The world in which persons find themselves is thus what I mean by 'the common'. I here assume that there is no great difficulty in identifying *clear* cases of persons and of non-persons, and that disputed cases (e.g., fetuses, animals) need not detain us here, since settling such disputes will not alter the principles with which we are now concerned, but only their application to the disputed cases.

The task at hand is that of identifying exactly which decisions about the common are properly subject to collective control. The discussion of the lake example shows that there are some, but a theoretical account is still needed. The account depends in part on a distinction between decisions 'about the common' and decisions 'about persons'; thus, this distinction needs to be made more precise. We can get at the distinction by considering more fully why it has significance from the respect-for-persons viewpoint.

The need for this distinction can be seen if we compare the discussion of the lake case with a case involving a decision as to what a person shall do. For example, consider the decision as to whether a particular woman, say, Mary, shall have sexual intercourse with a particular man, say, Tom. If we apply the reasoning used in the lake case to this example, it may appear that we should conclude that it is not a violation of respect for persons to impose a decision here which Mary opposes. To allow Mary to decide unilaterally (i.e., without the concurrence of any other person, including Tom) not to have sex with Tom, seems to give Mary more control than Tom, given that Tom wants to have sex with Mary. For then Mary is able to determine unilaterally whether Tom gets what he wants. Thus, it might seem that the best way to respect the control to which everyone is entitled would be to equalize it by allowing all interested parties to have an equal vote in making the decision. This would presumably at least involve Tom in the decision, and perhaps suggests that a collective decision would be called for. Nonetheless, there is no dispute about how this case should be handled. Mary should be allowed to decide unilaterally not to have sex with Tom, and our previous discussion of the personal sphere (Section 3.2) provides for this.

Why is this case different from the lake case? Why is the collective decision approach, which is so appealing in the lake case, so unappealing here? I submit that the two cases are examples of decisions which have an importantly different moral status. Some decisions are such that individuals must, morally speaking, be allowed to make them for themselves without the concurrence of others, while other decisions must be subject to collective control even if this has the effect of restricting individuals' choices for

themselves. Thus we need to determine what makes the lake case different
from Mary's case.

The decision about whether Mary shall have sex with Tom is *necessarily*
a decision about what a person shall do; the decision is *logically* inseparable
from a decision about what Mary shall do with her body or from a decision
about what shall happen to Mary's body. By contrast, the decision as to
whether the lake shall be one with uncontaminated water is *logically sepa-
rable* from decisions about what persons shall do; it is not in itself a decision
about persons. Its relationship to the activities of persons is not one of logic,
but of causation. A decision that the lake shall remain uncontaminated has
implications for the conduct of persons because of the causal relationship
which holds between certain conduct and the contamination of such things
as our lake. Dumping sewage into the lake is related to the lake's contamination only causally and not logically. If the causal relationships were different,
a decision that the lake shall be uncontaminated might have no implications
for the activities affected, given existing relationships. Thus, decisions may
be related to human activities in either of two ways. Some decisions are
inherently decisions about human beings, their bodies or their activities.
Reference to human beings is part of the meaning of such decisions. Other
decisions do not refer to human beings in this way, but refer to them only
indirectly because of the causal relationships which hold between the subject
of the decisions and the actions of persons. Let us refer to the former kind
as *decisions about persons*, or *person-decisions*. The decisions of the latter
kind with which we are concerned shall be referred to as *decisions about
the common*, or *common-decisions*.

Decisions about persons include all decisions as to whether or not any
specific person shall do or refrain from doing any specific action and all
decisions that all persons of a general class shall do or refrain from doing
actions. Thus, not only is the decision as to whether Mary shall have sex
with Tom a person-decision, but so, too, are decisions as to whether Mary
shall read a certain book, whether Mary shall sing, and whether Mary shall
have orange juice for breakfast. Other examples of decisions about persons
include decisions that no one shall engage in certain sex acts, decisions
that no one shall use certain substances in certain ways (e.g., drugs), and
decisions that all persons meeting a certain description shall report for
military service.

Decisions about the common include decisions similar to the one in the
lake example, decisions such as whether certain animals shall continue to
exist,[3] or whether a forest shall continue to stand. Decisions as to whether

and where to have a highway, a bridge, or a building would also be counted as common-decisions.

Does the distinction between person-decisions and common-decisions have moral significance, and, if so, why? We have some evidence that this distinction is morally significant in the judgments made concerning the lake example and the sex example. Insofar as we make opposite judgments about these two cases, we have such evidence since the former is a decision about the common and the latter is a decision about persons. Presumably we would make similar judgments about other examples of each of the two kinds of decisions. Further support for this conclusion can be obtained from a more direct examination of the distinction.

The basic commitment of respect-for-persons ethics leaves no doubt as to the proper assignment of decisions about persons. Persons must be allowed to control their lives, and decisions as to what happens to a person's body, and as to what a person shall do are decisions about that person's own life if anything is. Thus, for any given persons, that person is the one who must be allowed to decide what he or she shall do. Person-decisions, as such, may be interfered with only under the circumstances indicated by the harm principle, the principle of paternalism, and the welfare principle. In those circumstances the interference does not violate the principle of respect for persons. In the absence of such circumstances, the decision as to what a particular person does must be left to that person. Any other conclusion involves rejection of the basic idea of respect-for-persons ethics.

Decisions about the common differ from decisions about persons in that, qua decisions about the common, no person has any greater claim on the right to make them than any other person. Common-decisions, as such, do not point to anyone as the appropriate decision-maker. This is the basis of the moral distinction between person-decisions and common-decisions; the right to make person-decisions is assigned to the person who is the subject of the decision, while the right to make common-decisions cannot be so assigned. Nonetheless, caution must be used in drawing conclusions from this difference.

The need for caution is due to the fact that there is, as suggested earlier, a relationship between person-decisions and common-decisions. Someone's decision to engage in a certain activity also has the effect of being a decision to use a certain portion of the common for that activity; similarly, a decision that a part of the common shall be used or maintained in a certain way has the effect of being a decision that persons shall not engage in activities incompatible with that decision. Thus, if Tom decides to build a house on a particular location, he has made a decision which is both a person-decision and a common-decision, and if a community decides that its lake shall be free of sewage, it has made both a common-decision and a person-decision, because this is to decide that no person shall engage in the activity of dumping sewage in the lake. This relationship means that assignment of the right to make common-decisions is also assignment of the right to make certain person-decisions. If the right of persons to control their own lives is to be respected, this relationship must be carefully considered.

Let us focus on one quite ordinary example of this relationship: the decision of an individual, say, Joe, to eat an apple.[4] Joe's decision to eat this apple is both a person-decision and a common-decision. It is the former because it is a decision that Joe shall perform certain actions, viz, those involved in acquiring and consuming the apple; it is the latter because it determines the fate of one small portion of the common. That is, it determines that this apple shall no longer hang in its tree and, indeed, shall no longer exist as an apple. Now, viewing this as a person-decision, the foregoing argument suggests that Joe should be allowed to make the decision unilaterally; however, since this may also be seen as a common-decision, and since the right to make common-decisions has not yet been fully determined, it remains an open question whether Joe should still be allowed to make the decision unilaterally. Our tentative conclusion in the lake case suggests that perhaps he should not; however, that conclusion is not in fact appropriate for this case.

The mere fact that a person-decision has common-decision aspects is not sufficient to alter the conclusion that persons have the right to make such decisions unilaterally. The contrary view would cut far too deeply into the realm left to individual control. Consider, for example, the fact that human beings are always using the common in some way. One always occupies space somewhere, so that anything one does involves the common-decision that some portion of the common be occupied by oneself. The idea that this could be enough to make the decision as to where a person shall be physically located subject to anything beyond the person's own control is presumably quite unacceptable. Indeed, much the same could be said of Joe's decision to eat the apple; if decisions such as these were not to be left to the individual's unilateral control, only an extremely impoverished conception of a person's having control over his or her own life would remain.

There are also differences between common-decisions such as those just mentioned and ones similar to the lake example. That this is so can be seen by considering the applicability of the arguments used in the lake example to the apple-eating example. In the case of the lake, we saw that allowing each family to decide for itself whether to discharge sewage into the lake would have the effect of allowing these families who do not wish to preserve the lake to have control over the circumstances of families who want to save the lake. This differential control is not present in the apple-eating case. Allowing Joe to decide for himself whether or not to eat a particular apple does not give him control over the lives of others. Joe's decision to eat the apple does mean that others will not have this apple available for their own use, but — in the absence of special circumstnaces — this does not result in differential control, for there are other apples available for others. They may thus have apples if they want them, and allowing Joe to do as he pleases with this apple does not give him control over other people. Joe's consuming of the apple affects others, but only in a way which is an unavoidable result of living in a world with other persons.

The general implication of these observations is that many common-decisions are morally on a par with person-decisions and thus should be treated as such. In other words, many common-decisions as well as person-decisions belong in the personal sphere. These common-decisions share with person-decisions the characteristic of being free from the kind of objection made against the laissez-faire approach in the lake case, since neither involves the kind of differential control seen there. Further, allowing individual persons to have full, unilateral control is, from a respect-for-persons point of view, preferable to collective control within a certain sphere. While for lake-type cases collective control assures everyone some measure of control and avoids differential control, this is no advantage where Joe's decision to eat the apple is concerned. Joe has more control over his own life if he is allowed unilateral control over his own apple-eating decisions and none over those of others than if he and everyone else have an equal vote on everyone's apple-eating decisions. Person- and common-decisions of this kind are to be left to the unilateral control of individuals; the rationale for this is that full control over something is better than shared control over everything; to insist on shared control over everything would be to deny the moral significance of the separateness of persons, denial of which would be tant-amount to denial of respect-for-persons ethics itself.

What we have found, then, is that some decisions about the common are like person-decisions in that individuals may be allowed full, unilateral control over these decisions without the result that some persons have control over the lives of others. I shall refer to such common-decisions as *personalized common-decisions*, reflecting the fact that these decisions, while not themselves person-decisions, are like person-decisions in that they are to be left to individuals. These are to be contrasted with what I shall call *other-regarding common-decisions*. Other-regarding common-decisions are decisions about portions of the common which have an importance for the lives of others which goes beyond being merely another representative of a kind of decision in which others may take an interest. As we have noted, the effect one has on others through any appropriation of a portion of the common is simply a part of living in a world in which there are others. The fate of any portion of the common has this 'routine' effect on persons. However, when a portion of the common plays a more significant role in the lives of others, control over that part of the common becomes control over an aspect of the life of another. In these cases we have an other-regarding common-decision. Respect for persons does not require deference to the unilateral decisions of individuals when the decision is of this type.[5]

The apple-eating example is an instance of a more general class of common-decisions which are personalized. Human actions in many ways routinely involve decisions about the common, in that some particular portion of the common will be used in some way if the action is performed. In many such cases, the only effect the decision, qua common-decision, will have on others is that some particular portion of the common will no longer be available for their use. This will be so when the particular has no special characteristics which make it significantly distinguishable from other particulars of its kind. There are many other apples, for instance, not importantly different from the apple Joe chooses to eat. Joe's use of this particular portion of the common does not mean that others cannot have experiences equal in quality to the experience one of them could have had using the particular Joe has consumed. This mere routine importance which a portion of the common may have for others is not sufficient to make decisions concerning it other-regarding. Decisions about portions of the common with only routine importance for others are thus personalized common-decisions.

In classifying a particular common-decision as either personalized or other-regarding, the basic concept is that of other-regarding common-decisions; common-decisions are personalized when and only when they are not other-regarding. The test of other-regardingness is whether the portion or aspect of the common in question has more than routine importance for the lives of others. If others' opportunities or experiences with the common would be affected in more than the routine way, the decision is other-regarding.

This can be made more concrete by considering some of the common-decisions which are other-regarding.

There are several major types of other-regarding common-decisions which should be characterized here. The lake case is an example of a type of decisions I shall call *modification decisions*. These are decisions involving use or alteration of a particular part of the common which plays an established role in the lives of more than one person. The families living on the lake are accustomed to having it available for swimming and fishing as well as for sewage disposal; to change it by making it unfit for swimming and fishing would be to deprive them of experiences to which they are accustomed. Moreover, it is this particular lake which plays the established role in the lives of these families; even if there are other equally attractive lakes elsewhere, this one is special to these people because of the established relationship. Modification decisions are other-regarding since they have to do with particulars which are important for the lives of people not merely in the routine way described above, but through the established relationship. Modification of such a particular has more than the minimal, unavoidable effect on others associated with all uses of the common.

Elimination Decisions. Elimination decisions are decisions concerning particular parts of the common which represent unique examples of a kind. A particular apple is not a unique example of a kind since there are so many examples of that kind of thing; the last individual of a species, however, would be such an example. If the last bald eagle, for instance, were killed, the world would be altered not only in that there would be one less particular living thing, but also in that the world would no longer contain that *kind* of thing. A particular can thus acquire a special status as a unique representative of a kind. Elimination decisions – that is, decisions to alter or destroy a unique example of a kind – are other-regarding because such decisions alter the potential experiences available to others, not merely by reducing the number of instances of a kind available for others, but by eliminating the possibility of all experience-types which are dependent on the existence of instances of the kind. If, for example, I were to kill all the remaining bald eagles, I would be eliminating a range of possible experiences – those involving living bald eagles – for others, thus altering their circumstances in more than a routine way. Elimination decisions differ from modification decisions in that the latter have to do with particulars which play an established role in the experiences of others, while the former involve particulars which do not necessarily have such a role.

Site-Selection Decisions. In some circumstances it will be necessary to choose a site for some facility such as an airport or a highway which would be used by many persons. Such a site would not necessarily be a unique example of a kind nor would it necessarily be one which plays an established role in the lives of those who would use it, so its selection would fall under the headings of neither modification decisions nor elimination decisions. Despite the fact that the particular site is not uniquely important prior to its selection, the decision confers such a status upon the site; furthermore, the site is an example of a *kind* (e.g., sites suitable for airports or highways) which is of unique importance for the project in question. If such decisions were made unilaterally, then the one making the decision would be exerting control which affects the usefulness of the common for others in a way which goes beyond the routine. The very possibility of using the common in such ways could be ruled out if site-selection decisions could be unilaterally vetoed. Site-decision decisions are thus other-regarding.

Coordination Decisions. Suppose that two groups want to use the same field at the same time for two incompatible activities, e.g., football and baseball. Must the two groups as a whole (a collective) accept the results of the individual decisions of the various persons involved? To say that they must would mean that the field might not be used in a satisfactory way for either purpose, as would be the case if some of the individuals on each side insisted on going ahead with their respective game. In this situation, a portion of the common has been selected by different groups for incompatible activities. The site in question plays more than the minimal, routine role in the lives of the individuals involved, since it has been specifically chosen by them for their activities. A decision as to who gets to use the field when, would thus be an other-regarding common-decision. What is involved here is a matter of coordinating incompatible activities so that all may go on but at times and places which allow each to occur without interference from other activities. This coordination may be achieved through decisions as to which portions of the common shall be used for which activities at what times. These decisions are decisions about the common despite the fact that they refer to the activities of persons, for they do not *logically* entail decisions about what persons shall do. To designate, for example, that a particular field shall be used for football does not logically entail a restriction on anyone's activities nor does it require any positive action of anyone. It would not be incompatible with the decision to use a particular field, used as a football field, for baseball if no one wanted to use it for football at the time. Similarly, it would not be incompatible with the decision that a particular room, used as a reading room, be used for writing letters. On the other hand, using the room as a place to practice playing bagpipes would be incompatible with the reading room designation if anyone wanted to use it for reading. The point is that deciding that a particular space shall be reserved for a particular activity bars other activities from that space only if the other activities disrupt or otherwise causally interfere with the designated activity. Playing bagpipes interferes with reading while letter writing does not. Thus, the decision that a space shall be used for a particular activity is a common-decision despite the reference to the activities of persons. Coordination decisions are thus other-regarding common-decisions which provide for collective control over when and where incompatible activities take place, but not over whether they take place.

These kinds of decisions are not exhaustive of the sorts of decisions which may be other-regarding common-decisions, and a particular decision may manifest characteristics of more than one of these types. However, these types of decisions do represent major kinds of other-regarding common-decisions, and it is other-regarding common-decisions which are rightfully subject to collective control. We have seen several examples which support the claim that there is an important moral difference between, on the one hand, other-regarding common-decisions and, on the other, personalized common-decisions and person-decisions. The arguments which led us to favor collective control in those cases may now be seen to be applicable to other-regarding common-decisions as such.

Other-regarding common-decisions, again, are those decisions about the common which have to do with portions or aspects of the common which play more than a routine role in the lives of two or more persons. It is not possible to give everyone full unilateral control over such decisions, and since unilateral control by any person or persons not including everyone more than routinely affected would give some control over aspects of the lives of others, respect for persons requires that such unilateral decisions be subject to overrule by the decision of a collective composed of all who are more than routinely affected. Collective decision avoids the differential control, and since the portion or aspect of the common plays a role in the lives of more than one person, collective decision is the only means of assuring that each has some control over that aspect of his or her life. Collective decision best reflects the respect-for-persons commitment to everyone's having control over his or her own life.

It should perhaps be said that the argument for collective control over other-regarding common-decisions does not support the claim that it is *wrong* for an individual to unilaterally make such a decision; what the argument supports is the claim that it is *not wrong* for the collective to overrule the individual's decision in such cases. The individual's rights as a person are not being violated by such restrictions despite the fact that the individual would not necessarily be doing anything wrong in performing the action if there were not collective decision to the contrary. The unilateral making of an other-regarding common-decision is not in itself a violation of the principle of respect for persons.

At this point, let me provide a statement of the principle of legal coercion associated with these considerations. The *principle of community* is the following:

> It is not a violation of the principle of respect for persons to use legal coercion to enforce collective control over other-regarding common-decisions, provided that valid conventional assignments of control are not violated, and provided that no activity compatible with collective control is thereby denied all outlets.

The two qualifications contained in the principle require explanation.

Valid conventional assignments of control must not be violated. While not all decisions about the common are other-regarding, common-decisions can become other-regarding fairly easily. If the same portion of the common comes to have more than routine importance for two individuals, decisions with respect to that portion of the common are then other-regarding. This means that there is a potentially large degree of instability associated with the right to control particular portions of the common, for the importance of a given portion may vary over time. To reduce this instability, a society may adopt conventions which allow individuals to exert unilateral control over portions of the common despite the fact that the decisions in question may be other-regarding. Thus, for example, a society may adopt conventions which allow an individual unilateral control over a piece of land even if some others come to have a desire to use that land. Since rules governing land use are the result of other-regarding common-decisions, and since control over a particular piece of land may be just the sort of thing the rules were designed to cover, they should not be abandoned merely because decisions concerning a particular portion of the common become other-regarding in an additional way. Granting precedence to the general conventions is the only way to allow everyone participation in the other-regarding common-decision concerning the conditions and limits of land use. Further, society itself must respect its own conventions by not interfering with the unilateral control of persons who have acquired the right to it through conventional assignment.

The right to control what is conventionally assigned to one's control is simply part of the right to conduct a life of one's own choosing; some projects one might choose would be impossible or pointless if one could not be reasonably certain that one will retain control over portions of the common. Of course, collective decision may also set limits to conventional assignments of unilateral control to individuals. Some uses of land, for instance, might be excluded from the scope of a landowner's control, or the landowner's right to unilateral control might be contingent on the land's not being needed for public use. However, so long as no such conditions obtain, conventional assignments of control must be respected by the collective.

No activity compatible with collective control may be denied all outlets. This qualification is necessary to head off the possibility that control over the common might be used to prohibit activities which actually belong in the personal sphere. Suppose, for example, that an opponent of birth control argued that the substances of which birth control pills are made are portions of the common with more than routine importance for persons other than those using them for birth control purposes. Would, then, a collective decision against using these substances for birth control purposes be enforceable under the principle of community? If this rationale for prohibition were acceptable, it would be possible to interfere with many activities by denying the materials necessary to them; of course, this is not a legitimate use of the principle of community. It is not in fact the case that the portion of the common in question actually has more than routine importance for opponents of the related activities; the substances of which birth control pills are made do not in fact play a role in the lives of the typical birth control opponent; what may affect them are the activities of others, but these are not prohibitable under the principle of community. Decisions with respect to the particular substances being used to make birth control pills are thus not other-regarding, so the principle of community is inapplicable. That principle is applicable only where there is more than routine importance to *the portion of the common* with respect to which a decision is being made.

Another dimension of this qualification can be seen in an adaptation of the lake example. Suppose that the question is whether to use the lake for sailboats, for powerboats, or for both, and that the collective decision is that its use be restricted to sailboats. If the same decision were reached for all available bodies of water, this would have the effect of prohibiting the use of powerboats at all. However, the rationale for the principle of community does not warrant this application of it; the principle is designed to provide persons with participation in decisions about certain aspects of

the common, not about what activities others engage in. The right of participation in common-decisions can be preserved without allowing collective
decision as to whether persons engage in certain activities. This is done by
allowing collective decision only with respect to when and where an activity
is allowed, and not with respect to whether it is allowed. This restriction is
in force when the aim which brings the principle of community into play
can be sought without the complete prohibition of an activity. It must be
determined why the decision in question is an other-regarding common-
decision rather than a personalized one; if the aim so discovered can be
served without prohibition, then prohibition is not acceptable under the
principle. For example, the decision between powerboating and sailing
is other-regarding only because the lake is the desired site for both activities
and because the two activities are (we have supposed) seen as incompatible.
The perceived incompatibility of the activities makes the decision other-
regarding. That problem can be handled by separating the activities; no
prohibition of all powerboating is necessary to make it possible to have a
place for undisturbed sailing. Where an activity is compatible with collective
control of other-regarding decisions – as in this case – only regulation of
time and place can be acceptable under the principle of community. Certain
other activities – such as hunting the last members of an endangered species
– can be prohibited under the principle. This is true in cases in which the
factor which makes the decision other-regarding can be handled only through
prohibition. Preserving an endangered species cannot be accomplished if
killing of its only representative is permitted, so prohibition of such killing
is permissible under the principle of community.

The principle of community is thus the respect-for-persons standard
for what the law may be used to do with regard to decisions about the
common. Where decisions about the common are other-regarding, the law
may be used to enforce collective preference; where they are not other-
regarding, legal intervention can be justified only when it can be brought
under the other recognized principles of legal coercion. The principle of
community is vital for allowing persons control over their own lives in
special situations in which the failure to make collective decisions permits
choices of individuals to interfere with each other. It is the primary justifying
principle for environmental legislation which does not involve harm to persons
because it allows for collective decisions concerning how the environment
shall be used. It also provides a possible justification for zoning restrictions,
restrictions on offensive conduct, and for community projects generally.
Some applications are discussed further in Chapter Ten.

CHAPTER SEVEN

THE PRINCIPLE OF NECESSARY MEANS

7.1. INTRODUCTION

Thus far we have found that the principle of respect for persons supports four principles of legal coercion: the harm principle, the principle of paternalism, the principle of community, and the welfare principle. These principles are *primary* principles, while the principle of necessary means is a *secondary* principle. Primary principles are those which specify the aims which make the use of legal coercion acceptable or unacceptable; secondary principles are ones which qualify the application of primary principles.

Secondary principles are important in answering questions about how primary principles apply to certain kinds of legislative possibilities. The harm principle, for instance, permits use of coercive law to prevent persons from harming others. This sets no limit on the nature of the connection between some specific prohibition and the harm to be prevented. It would be compatible with this statement to say that an acceptable prohibition must directly prevent harm, but it would also be compatible to say that the prohibition may be merely intended to prevent harm. The relationship between a prohibition and the purpose which makes it acceptable requires further exploration. A statement of the appropriate boundaries serves to qualify the application of the primary principles, and thus constitutes a secondary principle.

Some attention to this issue is implicit in certain discussions of applications of principles of legal coercion. One example is Joel Feinberg's discussion of the question of how Mill's opposition to the enforcement of slavery contracts might be justified. Feinberg points out that there may be no objection in principle to selling oneself into slavery provided that the decision to do so is fully voluntary, but that permitting persons to do this involves the risk of some persons becoming enslaved against their wills. It may be impossible reliably to differentiate between those whose choices to become slaves are fully voluntary and those whose choices are not. Thus, one may argue against enforcement of slavery contracts on the ground that non-enforcement of all slavery contracts is the best way to ensure that no one becomes involuntarily enslaved.[1] Michael Bayles makes Feinberg's argument into a general standard intended to guide the application of paternalistic considerations. He argues that when the harm a person may bring to herself is involuntary, and thus not her fault, it is acceptable to restrict the liberty of others in order to prevent injury to her and others like her. Preventing some persons from involuntarily harming themselves may require prohibiting everyone from engaging in a certain activity or otherwise restricting the liberty of others.[2]

The implications of this sort of thinking are extensive. Feinberg and Bayles have applied it briefly to paternalistic legislation, but clearly wider use of the same arguments is possible. The general idea here is that in order to accomplish a legitimate goal, restrictions may be imposed which have no justification other than that they are a useful means for attainment of the goal. Applied to the harm principle, this would mean that a prohibition could be acceptable even if what is prohibited is harmless; so long as prohibiting the harmless activity is a means to preventing something which is harmful, it would be unobjectionable. In this way, legislation usually opposed by those who rely mainly on the harm principle might turn out to be justifiable. Unless this approach is limited in some way, a Devlin-like legal moralism could be brought under the harm principle, since, as Devlin might suggest, if too little of popular morality is enforced, people will more frequently harm others because they will feel that everyone else is getting away with immorality; we cannot reliably determine when that point is reached, so we may enforce popular morality as a means to preventing the real harms that might occur if we did not. Of course, this thinking also has similar implications when used in conjunction with paternalistic considerations, as in the following arguments. If we do not prohibit mountain climbing, some persons who do not realize how dangerous it is will be injured; therefore, we should prohibit all mountain climbing. Similarly, for welfare considerations it could be argued that we should require persons to aid others whenever it appears that there is any possibility that they might need aid, since by doing so we could ensure that no actual cases of need are ignored. In short, if use of this argument is not restricted in some way, virtually any kind of legislation could be brought under the few principles of legal coercion found to be acceptable.

From a respect-for-persons perspective, there is an additional cause for concern about the thinking represented in these arguments. The arguments seem dangerouly teleological. They allow persons' liberty to be restricted merely because doing so is a means to an approved goal. The man who wants to become a slave is not allowed to do so because prohibiting this will serve the interests of others. A person who wants to die to avoid a painful death might be denied that liberty because permitting it is not in the best interests of others who might be mistakenly euthanatized were euthanasia permitted.[3] Why is this not subject to the familiar objection raised against utilitarianism, that it is an unacceptable sacrifice of some for the benefit of others? It is admitted that some of the activities which could be prohibited under this approach are perfectly unobjectionable in themselves, so how can there be any justification for interfering with them? A respect-for-persons theory must take this problem seriously, for unless there is a *respect-for-persons* rationale for restricting innocent actions as a means to other goals, doing so must be condemned as a violation of persons' rights to control their own lives.

One possible response to these concerns is rejection of the thinking which raises them. The position could be adopted that it is not acceptable to interfere with liberty as a means to legitimate goals. But this approach would involve rejecting some kinds of laws which appear desirable and which are not particuarly controversial. We encountered some of these earlier (Section 2.2) in the form of laws prohibiting activities which are often dangerous but not always so. Using explosives without authorization or driving while intoxicated are examples of activities that frequently involve risk of harm to others, but not every instance of such activities necessarily does so. Therefore, to prohibit these activities under descriptions not all tokens of which are dangerous is to interfere with some actions which are not objectionable in themselves. Laws such as these thus could not be accepted unless some instrumental justification for legal coercion is allowed.

7.2. THE PRINCIPLE OF NECESSARY MEANS

There is a way to reconcile the thinking in question with the principle of respect for persons. Consider the situation of the person whose liberty is restricted in order to serve some goal approved by the principles of legal coercion. Suppose that it is a case of someone knowledgeable about the safe use of explosives who is prohibited from using them without some form of official authorization. This individual is denied the right to undertake a course of action (using explosives without official authorization) as a means to protecting the public from the unsafe use of explosives. How can interference with this individual's control over his own activities be justified? Suppose that he were given a choice of whether to have a requirement that no one use explosives without official authorization. Since without this requirement some persons would be subjected to risk of harm from unsafe use of explosives that could be avoided, refusal to accept the requirement involves a kind of disregard for the safety of others. That being the case, concern for the importance of others' having control over their own lives demands that the individual accept this restriction of his liberty; it is a limitation he must accept because it is reasonably regarded as necessary to safeguarding others' ability to function as persons. Since the individual is morally required to accept this limitation, there is no objection to the legal requirement that authorization be secured.

What we have here is an argument analogous to the argument for the welfare principle. In the case of the welfare principle positive actions are required because the failure to perform them involves a failure to act according to the moral importance of persons' controlling their own lives; here we see that this reasoning applies to acceptance of limitations on one's liberty as well. The relationship between the innocent activity and the safeguarding of the personal functioning of others provides the basis for the restriction. However, just as the welfare principle is subject to important qualifications, so too is instrumental justification of legal restrictions. For one thing, there is the limitation on the extent of the sacrifice which a person may be required to accept for the sake of others; no one can be required to make a major sacrifice of his or her own status as a person. This qualification allows instrumental justifications to avoid the objections made against teleological theories. Serious sacrifices cannot be required because the refusal to make such a sacrifice is not a failure to respect the moral importance of persons. So some things cannot be required of individuals even if requiring them would serve approved goals or lead to the best overall result. Thus, one of the concerns about instrumental thinking generally need not raise difficulties for the respect-for-persons use of that approach.

Second, there is the question of which aims are of sufficient importance to warrant interference with persons' liberty for merely instrumental reasons. In discussing the welfare principle, we saw that one is required to provide aid only when that is needed for someone's functioning as a person, and the same thinking also should apply here. However, our present concern is only with instrumental justifications as they apply to the principles of legal coercion previously discussed; thus, only a limited set of aims need be considered. Further, since the aims cited in the four primary principles of legal coercion are all based on protecting personhood, those aims serve as acceptable aims to be served by instrumental restrictions. In other words, the aims authorized by the principles of legal coercion are so related to functioning as persons that their pursuit is an acceptable goal for use of legal coercion involving prohibition of some particular actions unobjectionable in themselves.

Third, there is the question of the connection between restrictions on actions innocent in themselves and the promotion of aims approved by principles of legal coercion. If the restriction of innocent actions is to be justifiable, it must actually promote one or more of the legitimate aims of legal coercion. If, for instance, the aim in question is preventing persons from harming others, an acceptable restriction on innocent actions must actually be more effective in preventing harm than a similar restriction which does not interfere with innocent actions. Thus, if the aim of, say, a blanket prohibition of euthanasia is prevention of murders disguised as acts of euthanasia and prevention of killings mistakenly thought to be desired by the victims, then the prohibition is acceptable only if such harms are actually reduced by the prohibition. Otherwise, the interference with those who truly wish to end their own lives lacks justification, since on that condition there is no reason why they would be required to agree to the prohibition. Further, interference with innocent actions is justifiable only if there is no less restrictive way to accomplish the aims involved. Consider the possibility of prohibiting everyone from smoking in order to protect those who might unknowingly injure themselves by smoking. While a blanket prohibition on smoking might serve that aim, it could also be achieved by allowing smoking but making sure that everyone who smokes knows of the risks involved (e.g., such as with the warnings on each package which are presently required in the United States). Since this aim can be achieved through a means less restrictive than the blanket prohibition, the less restrictive means must be used. The ground for this claim is again that there is no reason why an individual in this situation must agree to the restriction; it is not necessary to others' personhood, so respect for the personhood of those who would be restricted demands that they not be.

At this point, these considerations may be consolidated into a more formal statement. Let us refer to the kind of legal restriction with which we are here concerned as *extra-inclusive legal requirements*. Extra-inclusive legal requirments are those legal prescriptions and proscriptions which restrict some actions that are not subject to legal control in virtue of their own characteristics; that is, they restrict some action tokens which cannot individually be brought under the primary principles of legal coercion.[4] Thus, a prohibition against selling oneself into slavery is extra-inclusive because it interferes with possible unencumbered decisions to become a slave. A prohibition against euthanasia is extra-inclusive because it interferes with unencumbered decisions to die. A prohibition against unauthorized use of explosives is extra-inclusive because it interferes with possible harmless uses of explosives, and a prohibition against all smoking is because it interferes with possible unencumbered decisions to smoke. Our concern in this section, then, is determination of when extra-inclusive legal requirements are justifiable. The relevant principle is the *principle of necessary means*:

> It is not a violation of the principle of respect for persons to use legal coercion to enforce extra-inclusive legal requirements, provided that the extra-inclusive requirement is necessary to the attainment of one or more of the legitimate aims of legal coercion (those indicated by the primary principles of legal coercion). and provided that the burden of the extra-inclusive requirement is fairly distributed and does not involve major sacrifice for anyone.

As we have seen, the rationale for the principle of necessary means is substantially the same as the rationale for the welfare principle. The principle of necessary means functions as a secondary principle, i.e., as one which guides the application of the primary principles of legal coercion.

7.3. SOME USES OF THE PRINCIPLE

The principle of necessary means will have a bearing on many kinds of legislation. It is of course always used in conjunction with one or more of the primary principles. In this section, several legislative possibilities are examined through the use of the principle of necessary means and some of the primary principles.

Consider first the case of compulsory social security programs in which persons are forced to contribute to a fund which is used to provide financial support for persons who are beyond a certain age. This can be seen as a case of paternalism, in that contributors are in effect required to save for their own retirement years, and are thus protected from their own inclinations to spend everything they make without regard for the more remote consequences. The trouble is that this clearly fails to be a sufficient justification for requiring everyone to participate in a social security system. There will be some individuals who, perhaps through personal wealth or private retirement programs, will have made sufficient provision for their own retirements and who would be taking no personal risk by not participating in the public system. Requiring everyone to participate would thus be extra-inclusive, bringing in the principle of necessary means. However, there is no apparent reason to think that requiring everyone to participate is necessary in order to protect from themselves persons who do need such protection, since it is clearly possible to identify some of those who do not need it. Thus, paternalistic considerations fail to justify required universal participation.

The failure of the paternalistic justification does not, however, show that required universal participation in social security cannot be justified, for other inclusionary grounds may be applicable. The most promising in this case is the welfare principle. Here there will be questions about whether the system can operate satisfactorily without universal participation (cf. Section 10.2). Arguably, the cost escalation which would result from less-than-universal participation would be such that either there would be insufficient funds to provide satisfactory support for all participants, or the cost of participation would be so high that not all who wanted to pariticipate could do so. In either case that would mean that there would be people in need of an important form of assistance (support in their old age). Since the duty to aid falls on people generally, the welfare principle provides a rationale for required universal participation. Thus, the answer to those who complain that they are capable of taking care of their later years on their own is not the denial of that claim, but the point that their pariticpation is a sacrifice they are required to make for the sake of those who otherwise could have no reliable support in old age. The fact that everyone will eventually recieve payments from the system only shows how insignificant the required sacrifice really is.

Another area of concern has been some of the regulations relating to highway safety. While some such regulations have obvious non-paternalistic grounds (e.g., speed laws help to protect people from becoming victims of the irresponsible driving of others), others do not. Laws requiring motorcyclists to wear helmets, which have been passed and then later repealed in several states, and laws requiring all drivers to wear seat belts, which are occasionally discussed, are examples, since such laws may be seen as protecting people from their own risky decisions not to use these protective devices. However, legitimate paternalistic grounds are insufficient for the justification of this sort of legislation. Motorcyclists who choose to go without helmets are generally aware of the view that they are safer with them, and in any case they can be made aware by use of licensing requirements involving the learning of such facts. Thus a lack of awareness of risk need not encumber the motorcyclist's decision. It might be argued, however, that a particular motorcyclist who was in fact going to have an accident on that ride was encumbered by his ignorance of that fact. This still is not sufficient for paternalistic justification. On the occasion of the decision to ride without a helmet, the intervenor would be as unaware of the upcoming accident as would be the rider, and so the intervenor would not *have evidence* of the encumbered nature of the decision not to wear the helmet. Further, an appeal to the general ignorance of the future which afflicts everyone's decisions will not support intervention either, for that sort of encumbrance never provides sufficient evidence of unencumbered consent to intervention.[5] Finally, since the method of informing people of the risks makes it possible for them to choose to wear helmets and thus protect themselves, legal intervention is not *necessary* for protecting those who will turn out to be injured, so the principle of necessary means does not apply. Legitimate paternalistic considerations therefore do not support such laws.

What about non-paternalistic justifications for such legislation? It is sometimes argued that society is justified in requiring helmets, seat belts, and the like for the sake of protecting itself against increases in hospital and other costs resulting from more frequent and more severe injuries. Superficially considered, it would seem that this is an argument based on the harm principle, since the argument suggests that the risk-taker harms society by imposing increased costs. However, the welfare principle is involved as well, since accidents impose costs on society only if society is required to aid accident victims. These complications may be set aside, however, for this type of legislation clearly involves the principle of necessary means. However we understand the aim involved, if it is pursued through a prohibition on the risky activity, it will be extra-inclusive. For instance, only a fraction of the total number of helmet-less motorcycle rides result in accidents, and only a portion of those are ones in which the helmet would have made a difference. Since the prohibition is extra-inclusive, it must be necessary to serving the purpose involved. Clearly prohibition is not necessary to the goal of reducing costs for society in general. Those who receive this sort of assistance can be readily identified and can be required to pay their own costs. Many will be able to do this through, e.g., personal wealth or insurance, and so their actions do not in fact impose a burden on society. Thus, the most that could be justified on these grounds would be some sort of limitation of the activity to those who can prove financial responsibility. The defensibility of even that type of limitation would be questionable because, for example, it seems to discriminate against the economically disadvantaged. While possible qualifications of this rationale could be discussed at length, this is perhaps sufficient to show that the rationale does not support a general prohibition on such activities as riding motorcycles without helmets.

Some contrast with the above cases may be seen through consideration of another prohibition sometimes seen as paternalistic, viz, the prohibition against active euthanasia. This can be seen as paternalistic in that it may serve to protect people from their own possibly irrational decisions to die. However, this type of legislation is also clearly extra-inclusive, since the possibility of an unencumbered decision to die cannot be ruled out. This can be seen perhaps most easily in cases of persons who would choose to be killed painlessly rather than endure a prolonged and agonizing process of dying from an incurable disease. If persons' control over their own lives is to be morally paramount, the possibility of justifiable active euthanasia must be recognized. Legalization of active euthanasia is another matter. The difficulty is that it may be impossible reliably to distinguish genuine cases of unencumbered decisions to die from spurious ones. An incompetent patient's family, perhaps motivated by a conscious or unconscious desire to avoid the burden of caring for the patient, could misrepresent his or her views on being in such a condition. Whether this was done knowingly or otherwise, the result could be erroneous assessments of the hypothetical unencumbered choices of incompetent patients. Even with competent persons, problems would arise. People might be pressured, in subtle or not-so-suble ways, into expressing consent to their own deaths. Others might consent because of a misguided sense of having a duty to do so. Lacking a procedure for sorting off such cases, allowing active euthanasia involves the risk that some will wrongfully be killed, and so a prohibition on all active euthanasia may be necessary in order to serve not only the paternalistic goal of protecting people from encumbered consent to death, but also the goal of protecting people from those who would take advantage of their vulnerability in order to get them out of the way. I do not mean to suggest that this is a conclusive case against the legalization of active euthanasia, for the matter deserves more extensive exploration than I have given it here. However, in these considerations we do have examples of the kinds of the things which require serious attention under the provisions of the principle of necessary means.

CHAPTER EIGHT

EXCLUSIONARY PRINCIPLES

8.1. INTRODUCTION

In addition to the distinction between primary and secondary principles, there is also an important distinction between *inclusionary* principles and *exclusionary* principles. Inclusionary principles state conditions under which uses of coercive law cannot be found in violation of the principle of respect for persons merely in virtue of being coercive; thus, they indicate what uses of law may be included in the sphere of acceptable uses. These are contrasted with exclusionary principles, which state conditions under which uses of law are in violation of the principle of respect for persons and thus are to be excluded. The principles of harm, paternalism, welfare, and community are all primary inclusionary principles, while the principle of necessary means is a secondary inclusionary principle. Primary inclusionary principles are at the heart of a theory of the proper uses of law, and, accordingly, most of the present work is devoted to them. However, exclusionary principles also play a vital role in the overall evaluation of legislation. There is a primary exclusionary principle, viz, that any coercive use of law is in violation of the principle of respect for persons if it is not authorized under inclusionary principles. There are also secondary exclusionary principles, and they qualify the application of inclusionary principles by excluding some uses of law that would be permitted were only inclusionary principles used. The use of secondary exclusionary principles may be illustrated through an examination of the issue of free speech.

8.2. THE PRINCIPLE OF FREE SPEECH

Freedom of speech or expression continues to be one of the topics frequently arising in discussions of the proper uses of law. The literature on these questions is vast and the number of different kinds of cases relating to free speech is large. Justice could be done to these matters only in a work primarily devoted to them; my aim here is merely to indicate the general approach to freedom of speech demanded by the theory of respect for persons and to illustrate through that discussion the role of secondary exclusionary principles.

Under the terms of the respect-for-persons theory of the proper uses of law, most speech cannot be interfered with because such interferences lack authorization under the inclusionary principles. It is relatively rare that interferences with speech will actually serve in the requisite manner the aims specified by those principles. Consider, for instance, interference with speech criticizing the government. Stopping such criticisim would not in each case prevent harm or serve other goals approved by primary inclusionary principles (except perhaps the principle of community, which is discussed further below), so a prohibition of speech of this kind would be extra-inclusive. However, only under quite extraordinary circumstances would the principle of necessary means authorize this sort of extra-inclusive law, for only under extraordinary circumstances would it be *necessary* to interfere with the speech to prevent harm or serve other approved aims. Under ordinary circumstances, the aims may be served by more direct means; acts of violence, for instance, which might follow upon the hearing or criticism of government can themselves be outlawed. Other aims which might motivate a government's desire to interfere with speech — e.g., a specific office-holder's desire to suppress revelations of his abuses — would have no standing under the principles of legal coercion. Insofar as interferences with speech are protected against because they fail to have authorization under the inclusionary principles, it is unnecessary to deal with speech as a case warranting special protection; in that event, interferences with speech would be dealt with in the same manner as any other interference.

However, some questionable interferences with speech could find authorization under the inclusionary principles. This is seen most easily in reference to the principle of community. That principle allows the use of legal coercion to enforce regulations as to the time and place of activities when the activities are found to be incompatible with other undertakings. These are simply coordination decisions. One can well imagine that speech advocating positions disliked by most members of a community might be seen as incompatible with the satisfactory performance of everyday activities, and that it would therefore be restricted. The view could be that people should not have to be subjected to hearing opinions they intensely dislike, and that could be seen as incompatible with everyday activities as much as would be, say, the presence of people in the nude. While complete prohibition of disapproved speech could not be justified under the principle of community, such speech could be restricted as to time and place, and there is nothing in the principle of community which would prevent such restrictions from being so severe that they would have the effect of denying unpopular opinions any opportunity for a meaningful audience. This suggests that speech may not be adequately protected by inclusionary principles.

This difficulty with speech is but one example of a type of situation which could arise in an indefinite number of ways. The inclusionary principles state aims which may be pursued by coercive means, but they set few *constraints* on the means which may be used in the pursuit of those aims. Since even admirable goals may sometimes be sought by objectionable means, there is a need for such constraints in a theory of the proper uses of law. There are various ways in which this need might be accommodated. Constraints could be built into the inclusionary principles, as the prohibition on major sacrifice is built into the welfare principle, or constraints could be stated in separate principles, and perhaps they could be handled in other ways as well. In the terms of the present theory, the use of separate principles seems preferable. While it might be possible to build all required constraints into the inclusionary principles, this would be likely to make them unduly cumbersome. Further, since some constraints are applicable to all the inclusionary principles, the use of separate principles avoids redundancy. I thus propose to accommodate this kind of constraint through the use of secondary exclusionary principles. These can best be explicated by consideration of a specific issue of this type, followed by discussion of extension to other areas. Let me then return to the issue of freedom of speech for this purpose.

We have seen that the principle of community might authorize in some cases fairly severe restrictions as to the time and place in which advocacy of unpopular ideas may be undertaken. Other inclusionary principles might also be used to support interferences with speech. Consider, for example, the case of the march of the American Nazis in Skokie, Illinois, which was prominent during 1977–78. Among the arguments intended to support prohibition of the march was the claim that doing so would prevent harm – the psychic harm which would be inflicted on the Jewish residents of Skokie who would have to endure advocacy of doctrines which had so adversely affected their lives, and perhaps also harm resulting from acts of violence provoked by the march.[1] Suppose that these harms are sufficient to authorize prohibition of the Nazi march under the harm principle. Does that mean that such prohibition is acceptable, or does speech (or, as in this case, an act which expresses opinion) merit special protection?

I shall argue that respect for persons demands that some forms of speech be given special protection over and above that which is afforded by the

requirement that legal coercion be used only when authorized under inclusionary principles (i.e., the primary exclusionary principle). This special
protection derives from the importance of communication for the participation of persons in collective decision-making. Briefly, the rationale is this.
We may assume that respect-for-persons ethics requires that the collective
decision-making process be democratic, in the sense that everyone is entitled
to participate in the process in some way that makes his or her decisions,
in conjunction with those of others, determinative of the outcome of the
process at some stage. To deny participation to some would be to deny them
a form of control over their own lives, and it would be to place those permitted participation in a position of control over the lives of those denied.
There is no apparent way to reconcile this with the principle of respect for
persons, and so I shall assume that a full-scale examination of political procedures from a respect-for-persons viewpoint would show that some form of
democracy is required. However, full participation in a collective decision-
making process requires both information and the right to present and defend
the positions one favors. Without information relevant to the assessment
of others' proposals and without information which would lead one to make
proposals, one cannot participate in the process in an unencumbered way.
Without the right to introduce proposals one favors, one lacks a kind of
participation granted to others. Thus, in suppressing the advocacy of even
false and vile doctrines, the suppressor takes steps which conflict with persons' rights to participate in collective decision-making. If the doctrines are
suppressed completely — not permitted to be presented at any place or time
— then their advocates have been denied a right which others have (i.e., the
right to present their positions), and others have been denied knowledge
which they may need for unencumbered decision-making. This does not
suppose that there may be any truth in the doctrines; the point is rather
that to suppress advocacy of falsehoods can be to deny persons knowledge of
the fact that some believe, or are willing to represent themselves as believing,
the falsehoods. Such knowledge could be crucial in planning countermeasures,
such as promulgation of evidence refuting the falsehoods or planning for
other problems which could result from some people's acceptance of them.
In short, those with the authority to make collective decisions — that is,
everyone — can perform that function properly only if they are aware of
what is taking place in their society; since suppression of the advocacy
of falsehoods can deny them this knowledge, it is unacceptable.

However, it might be argued that in the Skokie case there is no question
of complete suppression of Nazi doctrine. Even if public expression of

support for Nazism is not allowed in Skokie, it will be allowed elsewhere, and that may be sufficient to respect rights to participate in collective decision-making. The trouble with this argument is that it allows for prohibition of speech on grounds which do not preclude complete suppression. To allow a community to suppress speech because it finds the speech objectionable is to leave open the possibility that some speech will be deemed unacceptable in every community, thus resulting in its complete suppression. Restraints on speech could be acceptable only if based on a rationale which does not permit complete suppression.

This latter kind of case may be present in the following example. Suppose it is a matter of a speaker shouting Nazi slogans to an angry antisemitic crowd gathered outside the home of a Jewish family. Here the familiar language of the 'clear and present danger' seems appropriate. Prohibition of incitement in such circumstances could serve to prevent harm, but if interference is limited to cases in which there is a clear and present danger of harm, it is not allowed to result in complete suppression. The incitive views may be presented at another time, when there is no clear and present danger of harm. This could result in complete suppression only if there were views the expression of which always posed a clear and present danger of harm.

The hypothetical case of views which always pose a clear and present danger of harm warrants consideration. There may not be any realistic examples of this sort of thing, but the possibility should examined in order to make clearer the relationship of the principles we are now working with. In this hypothetical case, preventing harm can be accomplished only by the complete suppression of certain views, and thus at some cost to persons' rights to participate in collective decision-making (as argued above). To decide whether this is in violation of the principle of respect for persons, one must compare the specific harms in question with the specific threats to participation rights. The resolution which best reflects the commitment to the importance of persons' having control over their own lives would be the approach deemed correct under the principle of respect for persons. Thus, what is called for here is something approximating a 'balancing of interests'. That is, the decision must be made by looking at what is at stake on all sides in the specific case. Some harms, e.g., preventing loss of life, might be of sufficient importance to justify constraints on pariticpation rights, while other, lesser harms might not be. It should noted that this weighing of competing considerations is the proper procedure only in special cases in which different factors recognized as important under the principle of respect for persons appear to conflict with each other. In those cases an appeal back to the fundamental principle is necessary. Given enough such conflicts, it might be possible to develop principles to guide the treatment of such cases. That, however, is a matter for a work aimed primarily at free speech issues.

The rationale for the special protection of speech suggests that it may be appropriate to distinguish certain kinds of speech from others. The case for special protection applies to speech which has a bearing on collective decision-making, that is, to speech which may be called 'political speech'. It would seem that not all speech does have a bearing on collective decision-making. No one needs to express or hear tales of the average person's sex life, for instance, in order to participate in the political process. Thus, the arguments for special exclusionary protection appear to be inapplicable to some speech. This leaves room for laws against defamatory statements about individuals. Of course, I am leaving the distinction between political and nonpolitical speech rather intuitive; should this distinction ultimately prove to be unsatisfactory, that would mean that special protection must be extended to all speech. For present purposes, however, I will assume that the distinction is viable.

It should be emphasized that it does not follow from the claim that some speech merits no *special* protection that it merits *no* protection. The present theory provides protection for *all* speech in that no interference with speech is acceptable unless it falls under some inclusionary principle; *some* speech, i.e., political speech, is provided with additional protection. Thus, given the distinction between political and nonpolitical speech, there are two levels of protection for speech.

How do these considerations fit into the larger theoretical structure? It has been argued that at least some speech warrants special protection such that interference with it may be in violation of the principle of respect for persons despite the fact that the interference may be authorized by inclusionary principles. This qualification on the inclusionary principles serves to recognize that some uses of legal coercion are open to *prima facie* objections *in addition* to the objection that they are coercive. Prohibitions on speech are not only attempts to deny persons certain courses of action that they might choose, but are also interferences which threaten persons' rights to full participation in the political process. More generally, all uses of legal coercion are open to the objection that they wrongfully attach unwanted costs to some of a person's options for the purpose of securing compliance, simply because they are coercive; *some* uses of legal coercion are open to additional objections because of additional ways in which they violate, at least *prima facie*, the principle of respect for persons. The inclusionary principles of legal coercion are designed to indicate the conditions which must be satisfied if the coercive nature of a legal intervention is to be justified; when these conditions are satisfied, that is sufficient to overcome the objection that unwanted costs have been attached to certain options (the coercion objection). However, when additional objections also apply to a special kind of legal coercion, it can be justified only if it can be given a defense which is responsive to the special objections. That is, it must be shown that despite the additional objections, the use of legal coercion has sufficient importance to be deemed permissible under the principle of respect for persons.

In the case of freedom of speech, these factors may be summarized in a *principle of free speech*:

> Legal interferences with political speech are not reconciled with the principle of respect for persons merely because they are authorized by inclusionary principles, and they are impermissible unless defensible in ways which are responsive to the special importance of political speech.

Now I would not want it to be thought that I take this principle to be the solution to problems about freedom of speech, for I do not. In developing the principle, I have offered only a general indication of the kinds of interferences with speech that would seem to be justifiable or unjustifiable under the principle of respect for persons. Again, these are matters for a theory of free speech, and are of sufficient complexity to warrant discussion at length. The purpose of this principle is more limited in scope. The principle serves to indicate one of the boundaries of the application of the inclusionary principles by making it clear that interferences with political speech cannot be shown to be justifiable by the use of inclusionary principles alone; inclusionary principles are necessary for such justification, but not sufficient. The principle of free speech also indicates something about the kinds of reasons which would be sufficient, viz, that they must be reasons which are compelling even in the light of the special importance of political speech.

8.3. THE GENERALIZED EXCLUSIONARY PRINCIPLE

Having recognized this one area in which there are important objections to some uses of law in addition to the coercion objection, it will be apparent that there may be other areas in which special objections apply. For instance, laws which are racially discriminatory would presumably be open to challenge on respect-for-persons grounds because of the ways in which such laws may drastically reduce the options available to certain groups. Many such laws would not qualify under inclusionary principles, but even if some did, they could be challenged on the basis of the special impact they may have on the lives of persons. Other matters which would be likely subjects of secondary exclusionary principles are suggested by the sorts of things which receive special protection under the Bill of Rights of the U.S. Constitution. Wherever there are uses of law open to special objections beyond the coercion objection, a special exclusionary principle[2] could be formulated.

One could develop shorter or longer lists of these special exclusionary principles, but it will not be possible to develop a complete list. This is because it is not possible to anticipate all of the ways in which uses of law may become problematic from the respect-for-persons viewpoint. Instead, we tend to recognize special exclusionary considerations when our actual experiences show us that they are needed. It is our history that leads us to formulate exclusionary principles dealing with racial discrimination, but not with, say, discrimination based on hair color or eye color. Thus, formulating a truly complete list is not only impossible, but also not particularly desirable, since it would include many principles dealing with violations no one is tempted to commit.

In formulating a theory for handling historically important exclusionary concerns such as freedom of speech and racial discrimination, one must identify the reasons why the specific area warrants special protection, and then consider what grounds, if any, would justify intervention despite the need for special protection. I shall not explore these matters further for two reasons. One is that they are worthy of book-length treatment in themselves. The other is that our present concerns do not require it. The aim of this section has been to show that there are limits to what may be justified by inclusionary principles alone. That is accomplished by recognition of objections to legislation which are based on factors other than the coercive nature of the legislation. The inclusionary principles tell us what it takes to overcome the coercion objection, and that is the concern of this study. We must touch upon these exclusionary matters to guard against drawing unwarranted conclusions from the discussion of inclusionary principles.

The role of the various possible special exclusionary principles may be recognized in a general way. I propose to do this with the *generalized exclusionary principle*:

> Uses of legal coercion which are, *prima facie*, in violation of the principle of respect for persons for reasons other than that they are coercive are not shown to be justifiable merely because authorized by inclusionary principles, and are impermissible unless defensible in ways which are responsive to the specific *prima facie* objections involved.

This principle provides a comprehensive statement of the limits which were incorporated in the principle of free speech. It has two important functions. First, it makes it clear that only one kind of objection to law can be fully overcome by use of the inclusionary principles alone; second, it states that the only reasons which can overcome other kinds of objections are reasons which are of overriding importance even in the face of the specific objections involved. In other words, the job of justifying a piece of legislation is not necessarily over when it is brought under inclusionary principles. However, inclusionary principles do lie at the heart of what is required for the justification of legislation. All defensible uses of legal coercion must find authorization under the inclusionary principles, and many will fail on that ground. The present theory is devoted to that stage of evaluation, and thus reaches its limit when secondary exclusionary principles come into play. In this chapter we have seen, through the discussion of free speech, that there is a need for principles of this type, and we have seen how such principles fit into the larger framework.

CHAPTER NINE

PUNISHMENT

9.1. INTRODUCTION

The preceding chapters of this study develop a respect-for-persons theory of the proper uses of legal coercion. To a certain extent these considerations should stand or fall on their own merits. However, there is a seldom-discussed connection between the theory of the proper uses of law and the theory of punishment and other forms of coercion used to secure compliance with the law. Because of this connection, giving some attention to problems of the latter sort is desirable here.

The nature of the connection between discussions of the grounds and limits of legal coercion and discussions of punishment and other forms of coercion can be seen if we consider what is involved in claims of the former sort. Take, for instance, the claim that it is permissible legally to prohibit conduct harmful to others. Such a claim asserts that punishment[1] or some other form of coercion may be applied to the kind of conduct indicated, i.e., conduct harmful to others. Now punishment and other forms of coercion are controversial in that there are questions about whether they are justifiable; some would deny that any form of coercion is justifiable. If this extreme claim that no form of coercion is justifiable were correct, the claim that it is permissible to prohibit harmful conduct would be undermined, for legal prohibition has always involved coercion of one form or another. Speaking more generally, it will be seen that affirmative answers to the question "What kinds of conduct may be dealt with coercively?" logically presuppose that some forms of coercion may be used. In practice such answers have assumed that punishment may be used. Thus, in order to defend my claims that it is permissible to interfere coercively with certain kinds of conduct, I must show that at least one form of coercion may be used. Since punishment is the form of coercion most commonly presupposed in these discussions, and since it is the form of coercion in which philosophers have been most interested, attention to the problems of punishment is appropriate.

This connection between the theory of the proper uses of law and the theory of punishment has not been widely recognized. One seldom finds a discussion of either set of issues which addresses the other set at all. One reason why the connection may not have been seen could be that many treatments of questions about the proper uses of law are concerned only to discuss whether theoretical *limits* to the uses of law may be established. For instance, many discussions in this area have to do with the question of whether law may be used to enforce conventional morality. Now the claim that it is wrong to use law to enforce conventional morality does *not* pre-suppose the permissibility of punishment (or of other forms of coercion), nor do criticisms of the arguments used to back up such a claim. However, the attempt to explain *grounds for* legal coercion does involve one in the question about forms of coercion. The difference is that the negative claim that the law may not be used for certain purposes is logically compatible with the possibility that no forms of coercion are permissible, while the affirmation that coercive law may be used in specified ways is not. Since the present work attempts to establish both grounds for and limits to legal coercion, the defense of at least one form of coercion is necessary.

I shall approach these matters by considering the question of how punish-ment might be justified from a respect-for-persons perspective. Working from familiar theories of punishment, I shall suggest that it may be possible to adapt these to our present needs. Thus, my main concern is to bring together respect-for-persons theory and the theory of punishment in a defensible manner.

9.2. PUNISHMENT AND RESPECT FOR PERSONS

Perhaps the most influential recent treatment of punishment from an approach explicitly drawing on respect-for-persons considerations is that of Herbert Morris in his well-known article 'Persons and Punishment.'[2] Morris defends punishment as a system which is designed to ensure a fair distribution of benefits and burdens in a society. A fair system of rules provides benefits for everyone living under the system, but these benefits are made possible only through general acceptance of the burden of com-pliance with the rules. Those who violate the law accept the benefits of the system without making the sacrifice others have made, a sacrifice without which the benefits would not exist. The violator thus takes unfair advantage of the obedient, causing an unfair distribution of benefits and burdens. Punishment serves to correct this distribution by requiring the violator to accept a burden. Such a system, Morris argues, does not fail to treat the violator as a person. Unlike a thoroughly therapeutic system of dealing with offenders, punishment does not involve responding to persons in ways which are indifferent to their own choices or which regard them as not capable of rational choice. Further, punishment differs from wrongful coercion in that the rules of the system apply to everyone and equally distribute benefits and burdens; it also imposes burdens only on those who have chosen to deviate from normal conduct.[3]

Without suggesting that these considerations in favor of punishment are unsound as far as they go, I must argue that they do not go far enough. They are not sufficient to reconcile the use of punishment with the principle of respect for persons. Even if punishment differs from wrongful coercion in the ways Morris describes, that does not explain why threatening punishment is not a violation of persons' rights to control their own lives; it does not show why it is not simply a different kind of violation. The threat of punishment prevents persons from freely choosing certain options, and the actual imposition of punishment denies persons the right not to undergo whatever deprivation is involved. These objections to punishment are not met merely by pointing out that it is not as bad as other forms of wrongful coercion. What is needed is an explanation of why punishment is not subject to these objections.[4]

The claim that punishment is a system designed to distribute fairly benefits and burdens will be offered as part of this explanation. However, this, too, does not suffice. The fact that a system imposes benefits and burdens fairly does not show that it is justifiable to force someone to participate in the system. If a gangster forces all the businesses in his community to buy supplies from his company, he may be (in one straight-forward sense) imposing benefits and burdens equally within the community; everyone could be charged the same amounts and be given the same 'services'. Nonetheless, no one would claim that this equal distribution of benefits and burdens made the compulsory participation justifiable. Only a more sophisticated conception of fairness could possibly succeed here.

One possible ground for the notion that persons may be obligated to accept the sacrifices of such a system is the theory of political obligation based on the principle of fair play.[5] This principle states that by voluntarily accepting the benefits of a fair system of cooperation, one thereby acquires an obligation to do one's share in making those benefits possible. The difficulty here, however, is that the presuppositions of this theory simply do not hold.[6] The most obvious way in which this is the case is that there is no meaningful sense in which everyone *voluntarily* accepts these benefits; the difficulties involved in avoiding benefit from the system would, for many persons, simply be so great that their failure to do so cannot fairly be regarded as voluntary.[7] It is also not possible to rely on the notion that fully rational persons would voluntarily comply with this sort of institution, for, as I have argued in Chapter One, the principle of respect for persons requires respecting the unencumbered empirical choices of persons, not the choices of supposedly fully rational beings.

An adequate explanation of punishment, then, must include a defense of the way in which even a fair system of punishment may impose interferences on persons who have made no unenumbered empirical choice to submit to the system. How can it be justifiable to establish and use such an institution? My suggestion is that we look at how the principle of respect for persons handles the problem of violations of its own demands.

9.3. GENERAL JUSTIFYING AIM

Consider the situation in which one person, the aggressor, attempts to harm a second person, the victim. Assume that the aggressor's action violates the principle of respect for persons. In that event, one would be entitled to condemn the action as wrong or immoral. But does respect for persons permit *interference* with the wrongdoing? Recognition of a right to interfere would certainly be supported by the considered judgments of most, but there is a reason to be suspicious of that view. Interference is, after all, interference with a person's choices concerning the conduct of his or her own life. To be sure, the victim's life is also involved, but *why* is interference with the aggressor not simply a case of two wrongs not making a right? Why is anything more than passive resistance permissible?

These questions reveal two ways in which resistance to aggression may be viewed. One possibility – the *quietist* alternative – is that both the act of the aggressor and the act of the victim in resisting the aggressor are wrong because they are interferences with persons' control over their own lives. The second possibility – the *activist* alternative – is that while the aggressor's act is properly condemned as unjustifiable interference with a person, the victim's interference with the aggressor is permissible. It is not immediately apparent which view is required by respect for persons; I shall argue, however, that the activist alternative is supported.

The key to this argument is attention to the fact that respect for persons is a matter of recognizing the moral importance of *every* person's *having* control over his or her own life. This can be seen most clearly in a circumstance in which the aggressor dominates the victim over a period of time, as in a master-slave relationship. Deciding between the quietist and the activist is a matter of deciding whether to favor the right of control of the aggressor or the victim, since, given the aggressor's domination of the victim, both cannot actually have control over their own lives. In this context we can see that quietist view ignores the importance of *everyone's* having control. For if the victim is denied the right to resist, equality of control — that is, everyone's having control over his or her own life — is abandoned for the sake of protecting the control of only some. On the other hand, if resistance is permitted, the importance of equality of control is recognized and even the aggressor who may rightly be interfered with is granted no less control than others. Also worth emphasis is the point that respect for persons is a matter of respecting the importance of persons *having* control over their lives; it is not simply a matter of looking for equality of control as a *test* to determine whether or not some action is right. That persons have control over their lives *is* what is important, not merely an indicator of what is important. The quietist view suggests that what matters morally is not whether persons control their own lives, but whether they perform the actions permitted by a test based on whether actions respect persons' control. It is difficult to see any reason for being concerned with such a test if it is not the case that persons actually having control is what is fundamentally important. Only the activist alternative reflects this importance, and so I shall proceed on the asumption that defensive action may be taken against an aggressor even if that means interfering in some ways with the aggressor's control over his or her own life.

This right to take defensive action provides the basis for a respect-for-persons justification of punishment. It will of course not always be possible for everyone effectively to resist aggressors even when they are entitled to do so; direct interference with the attempt to do harm is only one kind of defensive resistance. Another is *punishment*. Insofar as punishment prevents actions violative of respect for persons, it is an additional means by which persons may attempt to resist aggressors. If successful, this method of defense would provide a person with protection against aggressors whose aggression could not be resisted directly; it would do so insofar as the threat of punishment deters offenders or potential offenders, and insofar as actual infliction of punishment incapacitates or reforms offenders. Since in these cases the offense is not attempted, but would have been attempted had punishment not been used or threatened, protection is provided by punishment. Now, provided that this sort of defensive measure does not violate the demands of respect for persons in other ways — that is, we must recognize that there are limits to the right of defensive resistance and that it is an open question whether the institution of punishment lies within those limits — we have a defense of punishment drawn from respect-for-persons grounds.

It will be apparent that the defense of punishment being developed here bears a strong resemblance to what has become the 'standard' view of the justification of punishment. The standard view calls for a distinction between the *institution* or *practice* of punishment, and applications of punishment to specific individuals; utilitarian considerations such as deterrence and incapacitation are said to be appropriate for justification of the institution of punishment while retributive considerations are said to be appropriate for justification of individual applications.[8] My view, like the standard view, appeals to the consequences of having punishment as a practice, and it also says, as does the standard view, that there are limits which must not be violated, and that these limits are not grounded in consequentialist considerations. There are also some important differences.

One weakness of many versions of the standard view is that they do not recognize the importance of non-utilitarian considerations at the institutional level.[9] The only only criteria provided for assessment at the institutional level are the utilitarian ones. The difficulty with this is that it allows no way to reject whatever happens to be the institution with the greatest utility. Suppose, for instance, that the 'therapy world' described by Herbert Morris[10] were the approach to harmful conduct with the greatest utility. Such conduct would be regarded in every case as symptomatic of disease and treated in a non-punitive therapeutic manner. Given effective modes of treatment, this could very well turn out to be the institution which maximizes happiness (or whatever). Now if *only* utilitarian considerations are relevant at the institutional level, then it is not possible even to *ask* the questions Morris asks about the therapy world, let alone reject that world on the basis of its impact on factors other than utility. In general, if only utilitarian considerations were relevant at the institutional level, there would be nothing to prevent institutions violative of respect for persons from being judged acceptable. Thus, an adequate account of the standard view must not ignore non-utilitarian considerations at the institutional level; the present respect-for-persons account has made (and will continue to make) use of the principle of respect for persons in evaluating possible institutions such as that of punishment.

A second contrast between the present account and most other accounts of the standard view is that the latter tend to view the utilitarian and Kantian considerations applied to punishment as drawn from independent and irreconcilable sources while the former does not. A pluralism of fundamental principles – one utilitarian and one Kantian – seems to be assumed; justifying punishment is then seen as a matter of showing how it can satisfy the demands of both of these competing viewpoints. The present account, however, makes use of only one fundamental principle, the principle of respect for persons. To be sure, the institution of punishment is defended on the basis of its expected consequences, but those consequences are relevant because of their relationship to the rights of persons. On the present view, punishment is seen as a means to the protection of persons' control over their own lives, not as means to the maximization of happiness or some other utilitarian value. Utilitarian considerations thus have a role derivative from the principle of respect for persons. This has several advantages. Monistic theories are favored over pluralistic ones by considerations of elegance and simplicity. Also, monistic theories do not face the problem of conflicts of fundamental principles, while pluralistic theories do. Finally, providing an account of punishment solely in terms of the principle of respect for persons serves one of the aims of the present study, that of demonstrating the capability of the principle of respect for persons for handling a broad range of ethical issues, especially those of normative legal philosophy.

Despite the use of some consequentialist arguments, the present theory remains deontological rather than teleological in its basic normative commitment. Teleological theories call for evaluation of the rightness of actions by reference to their results in promoting the good. Respect-for-persons ethics, as I have interpreted that viewpoint, calls for evaluation of the rightness of actions by reference to the actions' conformity to the view that persons' control over their own lives is of greatest moral importance. This is not a matter of maximizing control, since every person must be granted requisite control even if this results in less than the maximum possible amount of personal control. Further, evaluating the rightness of a particular action is not merely a matter of assessing the effects of the action on personal control. Thus, the present view is not subject to the standard objections to teleological normative theories. There remains a question, however, about whether the defense of punishment here provided is subject to some important objections applicable to utilitarian defenses of punishment. Dealing with these objections will serve to bolster the argument for the present view as well as to make the view more complete.

First, there is a question as to whether consequentialist defenses of punishment are subject to the objection that they use punishment of the guilty, and therefore the persons who are guilty, merely as a means to the prevention of offenses. If the only reason for punishing the guilty is that doing so prevents offenses, then, indeed, it would seem that the guilty are being sacrificed for the sake of the social benefit thereby obtained.[11] Thus, an adequate justification of punishment must include arguments in defense of that practice which do not appeal *solely* to its supposed beneficial consequences.

Second, an adequate defense of punishment must not only provide non-consequentialist arguments in defense of punishment of the guilty, it must also show that the consequentialist considerations used are not allowed to support punishment of the *innocent*. The charge that they support punishment of the innocent in certain possible cases is of course one of the main objections against consequentialist defenses of punishment. Any theory using consequentialist considerations in defense of punishment should be checked to be such that it is not open to this objection. Thus, an explanation of how the consequentalist considerations are limited to prevent this implication is in order.

Third, we must also give some attention to the problem of the severity of punishment. This is so not only because the severity question is part of any adequate theory of punishment, but also because that question generates still further possible difficulties for consequentialist theories of punishment. Consequentialist approaches to severity provide no guarantee that unreasonably severe punishments will not be called for in some circumstances. Thus, we must take care to see that the present theory does not also involve this difficulty.

9.4. DISTRIBUTION

The first two of these problems, explaining why the guilty may be punished, and why the innocent may not be punished, are best treated together. If the non-consequentialist explanation of punishment of the guilty does not include or apply to the innocent, then the first two objections will have been shown not to apply to the present theory. We must show, therefore, that the principle of respect for persons permits punishing the guilty, but only the guilty, for the sake of preventing further offenses.

Why should punishing the guilty be thought to be in violation of the principle of respect for persons? The main reason is the fact that the practice of punishing the guilty is intended to interfere with the control of the guilty over their own lives; those apprehended and convicted will be forced to pay some penalty they would choose not to undergo. While respect-for-persons ethics supports some use of defensive measures, punishment is problematic in that it involves inflicting some deprivation *after* the offender has committed an offense, and thus is a *defensive* measure only indirectly. Why, then, is it not a violation of respect for persons to punish *this* person so that *others* will commit fewer offenses?

I shall argue that it is permissible to punish for the sake of future benefits provided that two conditions are satisfied. First, the offender must have chosen to commit the offense knowing that doing so meant risking punishment. Second, the offense for which the offender is punished must be of a kind properly prohibited under the terms of the principles of legal coercion. When these conditions are satisfied, punishment does not violate the offender's right to control his or her own life.

The first condition — *the choice condition* — is essential because without it punishment clearly *would* be subject to respect-for-persons objections. If the condition is satisfied, then persons can control through their own choices whether or not they risk punishment; if punishment is used where the condition is not satisfied, then the infliction of suffering is not something brought on by the offenders themselves, but solely by the punishers without even minimal participation by the offenders. The offenders' control over their own lives is clearly denied in that event. Hence the necessity of the choice condition.[12]

The choice condition itself brings with it certain other conditions; that is, the choice condition cannot be satisfied unless other conditions are satisfied. The offender, for instance, must in some sense have the capacity to choose; if an offender lacks this capacity, it obviously would not be the case that the offender has chosen to risk punishment. This condition explains the relevance of many excuses which, if available to a given offender, would render punishment of that offender questionable. A second condition implicit in the choice condition is the requirement that punishment from a particular source — for our purposes, the law — cannot be justified unless the offender has had fair warning of the intent to punish actions of the kind in question. An offender who has not had a reasonable opportunity to learn of the law's plans to inflict punishment on those who engage in certain kinds of conduct cannot be said to have chosen to risk punishment. This means that the state could be justified in punishing only illegal actions, since promulgation of legal requirements is the means by which the state serves notice of its intent to punish certain kinds of actions. In general, then, the choice condition provides the basis for the explanation of the relevance of the offender's mental state to the justification of punishment.

The second condition — which I shall call the *content condition* — is that the punishment be for an offense for which prohibition is authorized under the principles of legal coercion. The importance of this condition may also be seen by considering cases in which it is not satisfied. Take, for instance, the standard 'gunman' situation. The gunman offers his victim a choice, e.g., 'Your money or your life!' Clearly, however, the fact that the victim is allowed to choose between these alternatives is not sufficient to make the gunman's action not a violation of the victim's right to control her own life. The reason is that the victim has the right to have *both* her money *and* her life, and the gunman has no right to force her to choose between them. Now the same considerations apply to the state, for the state imposes a choice on its citizens: "either avoid prohibited conduct C or we will inflict some deprivation upon you". If the citizens have a moral right to *both* engage in C *and* not suffer deprivation, then the state fails to respect citizens' rights to control their own lives, and the principle of respect for persons is violated. Everything thus depends upon whether the state has the right to interfere with the kind of conduct for which punishment is to be imposed, for if it does not, the forced choice set up by the state is unjustifiable. This brings in the principles of legal coercion, for those principles define the conditions under which it is acceptable for the state to interfere with various kinds of conduct. Interferences authorized by the principles do not violate respect for persons. Thus, when these kinds of conduct are involved, the state's imposition of a choice between the conduct and punishment does not violate respect for persons, for the state has the right to interfere in the kind of conduct disallowed. Hence the need for the content condition.[13]

Use of punishment of the guilty for defensive purposes is thus not a violation of respect for persons provided that both the choice condition and the content condition are satisfied. It follows from this that punishment of the innocent cannot be justified in the present theory, since such punishment would not satisfy either of these conditions and thus would violate respect for persons. The innocent do not choose to risk punishment, nor do they engage in conduct with which the state is entitled to interfere. Thus, the present theory can explain why it is permissible to punish the guilty and why it is not permissible to punish the innocent, and can do so by appealing solely to the principle of respect for persons.

9.5. SEVERITY

It remains for us to consider the problem of severity of punishment. It would be natural to adopt a consequentialist approach to the severity question, since the present theory makes the positive case for punishment depend upon the consequences of that practice. The consequentialist approach to severity calls for a comparative cost-benefit analysis to determine the appropriate penalty for each type of offense. The appropriate penalty is the one which will result in the best overall consequences, where these are measured by subtracting the costs of the adoption of each penalty from the benefits obtained therefrom. For purposes of these comparisons, the central costs would be the suffering imposed upon the offender and the expense of administering the punishment; the central benefits would be found in the offenses which would be prevented because of the punishment – those which will not occur because of the deterrence, incapacitation, and reform effects of punishment. Since punishment is justifiable only if it produces enough of these results to make it worth the cost, setting penalties in this consequentialist manner initially seems plausible.

However, this approach is subject to an objection which, if valid, renders it unacceptable to any but a thoroughgoing consequentialist theory. The problem is that this view seems to permit the use of very severe penalties for quite trivial offenses. If it takes a very severe penalty to prevent a trivial offense, it is charged, then the consequentialist approach demands the severe penalty. The consequentialist response to this objection is that it ignores the costs associated with use of the severe penalty.[14] The benefits obtained by preventing trivial offenses will not be sufficient to outweigh the costs involved. Hence, it is replied, the objection is not valid.

This consequentialist response is not adequate. Its weakness stems from a failure to attend to all of the factors relevant to the cost-benefit comparison. The relative benefits obtained by attaching a particular penalty to a particular type of behavior will be equivalent to the average amount of (let us say) disutility involved in each occurrence of that type of behavior *weighted* by the number of such occurrences prevented by the use of that penalty; the relative costs of each possible penalty will be equivalent to the average disutility associated with each actual imposition of the penalty *weighted* by the number of times the penalty is actually imposed. Thus, in the event that attaching a severe penalty to a trivial offense proved to be a very effective, but not totally effective, deterrent, the consequentialist approach could call for its use. The benefits obtained from deterring a large number of trivial offenses could very well outweigh the costs of a small number of uses of a severe penalty. The aforementioned consequentialist reply fails to realize that the costs of severe penalty can be minimal if it is used only rarely. The objection, therefore, is valid; the consequentialist approach fails to guarantee that severe penalties will not be attached to trivial offenses.

The most promising alternative to the consequentialist approach to the severity question is the retributivist's use of proportionality. This view would have the amount of punishment be proportional to the seriousness of the offense. It is preferable to the retributivist's *lex talionis* – an eye for an eye – approach because the latter lacks general applicability.[15] The difficulty with the proportionality approach is that it seems to rely on unexplained intuitions concerning which penalties are proportional to which offenses. Nonetheless, while it may not be possible to fully eliminate the apparent arbitrariness of this view, I shall argue that it can be made plausible by considering its role in a respect-for-persons approach to severity.

I have argued that, from a respect-for-persons point of view, the license to punish derives in part from the way in which punishment may serve as a defensive measure; the justification of punishment depends upon the assumption that it is at least somewhat effective in preventing offenses. Since punishment is a defensive measure, its use is appropriately guided by the kinds of considerations relevant to evaluating other kinds of defensive measures. It is clear that proportionality plays a role in the justifiability of individual acts of self-defense; an individual's defensive acts must not be harmful to an extent disproportionate to the seriousness of the threat to that individual. Thus, the use of deadly force in self-defense, if permissible at all, is permissible only to defend oneself against very serious threats; similarly, one would be justified in using only very limited measures to defend oneself against, say, having one's toes stepped on. If these features of individual self-defense can be explained, it may be possible to adapt the explanation to the problem of the severity of punishment.

In our earlier discussion of the welfare principle,[16] we saw that while a person could be in violation of the principle of respect for persons if he or she refused to endure a moderate or trivial sacrifice for the sake of preserving the life of another, that is not the case where the sacrifice involved is major. A person is not required to endure a major sacrifice for the sake of another, because the failure to do so is not a failure to recognize the moral importance of persons. The principle of respect for persons does not, in itself, favor one life over another, so in circumstances where a choice between lives must be made, it is not in itself a violation of the principle to choose one's own life over that of another.[17] Thus, the principle of respect for persons does not prohibit the imposition upon another of major sacrifice when this is necessary to protect oneself against major sacrifice. Here we have the beginnings of an explanation of proportionality in self-defense. While one may impose major sacrifice in order to protect oneself against major sacrifice, one may not impose major sacrifice to protect against moderate or trivial sacrifice, since the latter would be a failure to respect the supreme importance of persons' having control over their own lives. However, there is no reason in this to object to the imposition of moderate sacrifice to protect against moderate sacrifice. Similarly, no more than a trivial sacrifice may be imposed to protect against trivial sacrifice.

The general procedure suggested here, then, calls for recognition that the principle of respect for persons permits the use of the most serious defensive measures only to protect against the most serious threats, and that less serious threats warrant only less serious defensive measures. A rough ordering is accomplished by beginning with the matching of the most serious defensive measure with the most serious threats, and by then moving down the two scales (defensive measures and threats), allowing the cross-scale comparisons to be determined by relative 'distance' from the original cross-scale match-up indicated above. This approach will not, of course, remove all appearances of arbitrariness in matching defenses with threats, but it does provide an explanation of why grossly disproportionate defensive measures are unacceptable, and it does so by showing how some use of proportionality is derivable from the principle of respect for persons.

Attention to one further feature of the evaluation of defensive measures will also be useful. I have argued that there is no violation of respect for persons inherent in the imposition of major sacrifice on another for the sake of protecting oneself against major sacrifice; however, such an imposition would be unacceptable if it were not necessary for self-protection. The reason is obvious. Suppose, for instance, one's life were threatened, but that one could end the threat either by killing someone else or by physically restraining him. In such an instance, killing the person would be a failure to respect the moral importance of persons. Protection of life warrants imposition of major sacrifice only when necessary for that purpose. If we may generalize from this, the result is that not only must a defensive measure not be disproportionately serious, but it also must not be more serious than necessary to protect what is threatened.

Since, on the present view, punishment is justifiable in part because it is or may be a defensive measure, these considerations should also be applicable to the use of punishment. Proportionality requires that the amount of punishment not be disproportionately greater than the seriousness of the offense; thus, just as it would not be acceptable to impose major sacrifice to defend oneself directly against moderate loss, it would not be acceptable to impose major sacrifice as punishment in order to protect oneself indirectly against moderate loss. While this does not make things very precise, it does explain something the consequentialist approach to severity cannot explain, namely, why the use of severe penalties for trivial offenses is unacceptable in principle. Further, things can be made somewhat more precise by use of the requirement that defensive measures be no more severe than necessary to accomplish their aim; applied to punishment, this makes a place for consequentialist thinking about severity. Punishment should be no more severe than necessary to prevent offenses, or, more accurately, the penalty for a given offense should be no more severe than is necessary to prevent that kind of offense. Thus, if a point is reached where increasing the severity of the punishment for an offense fails to bring about additional preventive effects, then more severe punishments for that offense are unacceptable. Respect-for-persons theory of punishment therefore provides two upper bounds on the severity of punishment: punishment should be no more severe than is proportional to the seriousness of the offense, and no more severe than is necessary to minimize the likelihood that the offense will be committed.

Many question about punishment remain. However, if the preceding discussion is sound, the purpose for which it was undertaken will have been accomplished. That is, it will have been shown that at least one form of coercion can be consistent with the principle of respect for persons, and thus is permissible. This is sufficient to prevent the foregoing claims about grounds for legal coercion from being undermined by charges that no form of coercion is defensible.

CHAPTER TEN

EVALUATING LEGISLATION

10.1. THE PRINCIPLES OF LEGAL COERCION

The theoretical framework is now in place. In this section the various principles are brought together in a way which summarizes conclusions reached in preceding chapters and which indicates further how the principles may be used in the evaluation of legislation.

At the foundation of the theory is a principle expressing an essentially Kantian conception of the moral importance of persons:

> *The principle of respect for persons*: all actions must be consistent with recognition of the supreme moral importance of each person's having control over his or her own life in accordance with his or her own unencumbered choices.

Grounded in this principle is a set of further principles which express the demands of the basic principle in regard to various matters involving the use of legal coercion. These further principles are the *principles of legal coercion*. Initially we have:

> *The primary exclusionary principle*: it is a violation of the principle of respect for persons to use legal coercion in ways not authorized by the inclusionary principles of legal coercion.

This principle tells us that we must reject coercive uses of law which lack positive justification in inclusionary principles.

Positive justification must be found, first, in one or more of the *primary inclusionary principles*:

> *The harm principle*: it is not a violation of the principle of respect for persons to use coercive law to prevent persons from performing actions which violate the personal spheres of other persons.

> *The principle of paternalism*: paternalistic interventions do not violate the principle of respect for persons if and only if (i)

129

there is good evidence that the decisions with respect to which the person is to be coerced are encumbered, and (ii) there is good evidence that this person's decisions would be supportive of the paternalistic intervention if they were not encumbered.

The principle of community: it is not a violation of the principle of respect for persons to use legal coercion to enforce collective control over other-regarding common-decisions, provided that valid conventional assignments of control are not violated, and provided that no activity compatible with collective control is thereby denied all outlets.

The welfare principle: it is not a violation of the principle of respect for persons to use legal coercion to require persons to aid others, provided that what is required is (or is quite likely to be) vital to the personal functioning (functioning as persons) of those aided, and provided that the burden of bringing aid is fairly distributed and does not impose a major sacrifice on anyone.

When the use of legal coercion is question is extra-inclusive, it must also be examined in light of this *secondary inclusionary principle*:

The principle of necessary means: it is not a violation of the principle of respect for persons to use legal coercion to enforce extra-inclusive legal requirements, provided that the extra-inclusive requirement is necessary to the attainment of one or more of the legitimate aims of legal coercion (those indicated by the primary principles of legal coercion), and provided that the burden of the extra-inclusive requirement is fairly distributed and does not involve major sacrifice for anyone.

Any use of legal coercion which cannot be justified under the provisions of the above inclusionary principles — as stipulated by the primary inclusionary principle — is in violation of the principle of respect for persons. Any use which is permitted by these principles is no longer open to the charge of being in violation of the principle of respect for persons in virtue of its coercive character. These principles are thus necessary and sufficient for moral justification of the coercive dimension of law.

However, we have also seen that specific uses of legal coercion may come into conflict with the principle of respect for persons for reasons other than their coercive character. Accordingly, legislation which is authorized under inclusionary principles must be evaluated in light of this *secondary exclusionary principle*:

> *The generalized exclusionary principle*: uses of legal coercion which are, *prima facie*, in violation of the principle of respect for persons for reasons other than that they are coercive are not shown to be justifiable merely because authorized by inclusionary principles, and are impermissible unless defensible in ways which are responsive to the specific *prima facie* objections involved.

This principle is made more specific through the development of *special exclusionary principles*, which describe uses of law which have been found objectionable in some additional way. These include:

> *The principle of free speech*: legal interferences with political speech are not reconciled with the principle of respect for persons merely because they are authorized by inclusionary principles, and they are impermissible unless defensible in ways which are responsive to the special importance of political speech.

They also include whatever other principles serve to express experiences with ways in which uses of law can fail to meet the demands of respect for persons. When these principles apply, the discussion moves to theoretical concerns specific to the special exclusionary principle involved, and beyond the scope of the present theory.

The function of the inclusionary principles can now be further explicated through discussion of their application to some uses of coercive law.

10.2. TAXATION AND THE PROVISION OF PUBLIC GOODS

Certain benefits or services that may be provided by law have an irreducibly 'public' aspect, and these 'public goods' require special consideration. A 'public good' may be defined as "any good such that, if any person X_i in a group $X_1, \ldots, X_i, \ldots X_n$ consumes it, it cannot feasibly be withheld from the others in that group".[1] Typical examples of public goods are such things as police and fire protection, national defense, public parks, publicly financed insurance programs, and clean air. A difficulty raised by public goods is that they often cannot be provided through voluntary cooperation because the interest of each individual in the group is best served by not voluntarily contributing to making the good possible. If enough others make the sacrifice necessary to provide the good, then it will be available to the individual whether or not he or she makes a similar sacrifice (since it is public good), so it is not then in that individual's interest to make the sacrifice. Of course, if others do not make the necessary sacrifice, then, for most situations, one's own sacrifice will not be sufficient to provide the good. Thus, whatever others do, it is in each individual's interest not to cooperate voluntarily in providing public goods.

This characteristic of public goods is often taken as providing a reason for the use of coercion as a means of providing them. Public goods, it may be argued, cannot be provided without coercion which makes it in each individual's interest to cooperate; hence, coercion must be used. Coercion is thus taken by some as a 'solution' to the problem of providing public goods.[2] However, for our purposes, it is this 'solution' which presents the problem. The mere fact that a good cannot be provided without coercion cannot be taken by respect-for-persons ethics as a sufficient justification for the use of coercion, for on this view coercion can be justified only by showing the coercion necessary to persons' unencumbered control over their own lives. Even showing that the good is in each person's interest is not sufficient, for persons are not morally required to accept things merely because they are in their interests. Thus, for the project at hand, the difficulty raised by public goods is that of justifying the coercion which may be necessary for their provision.

One implication of respect-for-persons ethics is that there can be no comprehensive justification for coercively providing some public goods. There is no justification for coercively providing something merely because it is a public good. In other words, there is no justification for using coercion to provide some public goods. This is because justifying coercion requires showing that it will serve one of the purposes authorized by the inclusionary principles of legal coercion. Hence, for each public good, it must be shown that one or more of these principles warrants the use of coercion to provide the good; we cannot assume that this is possible for everything which may fit the definition of public goods. Thus, I shall approach this problem by examining instances of public goods which fall under various inclusionary principles.

Public parks are usually thought to be public goods, and providing for them may serve us as one example.[3] The principle of community offers the most promising starting point for this public good, since the question of whether or not to use a particular area as a park is a decision about the use of the common. Even if the area in question is private property, and the owner does not wish to give it up, the collective decision to make it a park may be enforced so long as the owner's claim to it may be understood to have been contingent on its not being needed for collective use. So the principle of community directly provides justification for the decision to set aside some areas to be left more or less in their natural state. What is not so clearly brought under the principle of community is any compulsory taxation which may be used to finance either the purchase or the development of the park. Why should persons who do not wish to have or use the park be required to contribute to it?

Justification of compulsory taxation to support the park requires that the principle of community be supplemented by the principle of necessary means. To require everyone to pay in support of the park is to impose an extra-inclusive requirement, since it is not the case that each individual's failure to contribute to the park is objectionable on its own merits. Assuming that the taxation scheme is fair and imposes no major sacrifice on anyone, the main question is whether the coercion is necessary; if it is necessary to effecting a collective decision concerning the common, then it does not violate the principle of respect for persons. However, it is not obvious that compulsory financing of public parks is necessary, since it would seem possible to require payment from only those who do wish to have or use the park. Perhaps voluntary contributions could get the project started and, once underway, admission could be charged anyone who wanted to use the park but had not contributed a fair share.

Joel Feinberg describes a rationale which might be used to show the necessity for coercion in situations such as this:

Suppose, however, the city charges only those who wish to use the park, and that this group constitutes 90 percent of the population. The richest 10 percent opt out, thus raising the average costs to the remainder. That rise, in turn, forces some of the 90 percent to withdraw, thus raising the cost to the others, forcing still more to drop out, and so on. This process will continue until either a very expensive equilibrium is reached, or, what is more likely, the whole project collapses.[4]

This argument does make it less clear that compulsory taxation would not be necessary, but it leaves open a possibility that requires closer examination, viz, the possibility that a "very expensive equilibrium" might be reached. Suppose that this happens so that the park is provided but only at high cost to only a fraction of those who would like to use it. This would seem to show that compulsory financing is *not* necessary to having the park.

However, why would even those who think the park is worth the high cost be willing to contribute voluntarily to it? If their contributions, individually considered, do not make the difference between having the park and not having it, then they have no incentive to contribute because the park will be available for their use whether they contribute or not. Of course, an incentive to contribute would be provided if access to the park were limited to those who contribute to it; then those who think the park worth the price would have reason to contribute even if not forced to do so. Thus, it again appears that compulsory financing is not necessary for the park.

Here the question may be raised of whether the park as now envisioned has the same character as the park originally conceived. The park which may be provided through voluntary contributions is one to which access is restricted, while the original conception may have been of a park freely available to everyone. It may not be possible to provide the latter sort of park without compulsory financing, for the very nature of the park precludes use of the incentives which make voluntary financing workable. So long as one's own contribution does not make the difference between having the park or not, one has no self-interested reason to contribute voluntarily to it. Therefore, compulsory financing may well be necessary for an unrestricted park.

Can collective control over the common be construed in such a way that it is sensitive to the difference between a park with restricted access and one without? It seems to me that it can. There is no reason why there could not be a collective preference that a particular area be available to all without restricted access; it may simply be the collective preference that the area be used in that way. If the persons expressing this preference are sensitive to the difference between free access and limited access, then so too is collective control over the common. Therefore, giving effect to collective control over the common may require compulsory financing for such things as public parks, and since this is necessary to a purpose authorized by the primary principles of legal coercion, it is permitted by the principle of necessary means so long as the burden is fairly distributed and does not involve major sacrifice for anyone.

This argument can be generalized up to a point. It will apply only in cases in which the decision to provide a public good is an other-regarding common-decision. It would apply therefore to such decisions as whether to have an interstate highway system or a public museum, but not to decisions that Johnny Carson or Luciano Pavarotti shall appear on television, since the latter are person-decisions. It also must be the case that the compulsory financing is necessary to providing the public good in its desired form. In determining such necessity, attention to cost escalation factors such as mentioned in the case of the park would of course be relevant. When these conditions as well as the other provisions of the principles of community and necessary means are satisfied, there is no objection of moral principle to the use of coercion to provide public goods.

Provision of some public goods can also be brought under inclusionary principles in addition to the principle of community. The protection provided by a properly functioning police force, for example, could fall under the welfare principle, given the circumstances of most actual societies. To the extent that police protection is necessary for preventing people from becoming victims of serious crimes, either through direct intervention in criminal attempts or through deterrence, it may be a vital form of assistance. Insofar as there is a segment of society which lacks the means for providing this protection for themselves, its provision would then be a form of assistance required under the welfare principle, and the burden of financing it would fall on everyone. Even those who would be willing to do without police protection for themselves would share in the duty to provide it for these others. Moreover, given the likelihood of cost escalation if some were permitted to forego paying for this service, it is likely that many would be unable to afford such services if participation were voluntary.

10.3. VICTIMLESS CRIMES AND THE ENFORCEMENT OF POPULAR MORALITY: PORNOGRAPHY

One practical implication which may be common to all views on law which might be called limits theses is opposition to the enforcement of popular morality and to the creation of 'victimless crimes'. The present thesis shares this opposition and thus explanation of the opposition will serve to show how the present thesis is a limits thesis. In general, it will be one claim of a limits thesis that legal coercion should not be used to interfere with conduct which does not victimize anyone, and the fact that a piece of behavior lacks a victim is taken to show that it should not be interfered with. However, in view of the preceding adoption of the principle of necessary means, this approach is unattractive, since that principle permits interfering with some conduct instances of which may harm no one where that is a necessary means to prevention of recognized harm. Thus, I prefer to think of victimless crimes as illegal conduct prohibition of which is not warranted under the inclusionary principles of legal coercion; identification of victimless crimes is thus a matter of determining whether interference with a specific kind of conduct may be brought under these principles. To make discussion of victimless crimes concrete, we must consider some specific, possibly victimless, crime. I shall discuss prohibition of the sale of pornography, and I shall assume that this discussion will suffice to indicate the direction to be taken in dealing with other kinds of victimless crime.

The term 'pornography' is here intended to refer to books, magazines, photographs, movies, etc., which describe or depict activities of a sex-related nature and which are primarily intended to arouse, or primarily have the effect of arousing sexual desire. I deliberately use the term in a broad sense so as to include virtually everything which advocates of the censorship of pornography are likely to be concerned about. Since on the present view something's being pornographic does not suffice to show it prohibitable, this should pose no difficulty.

In what ways, then, may legal coercion be used to interfere with the sale of pornography without violating the principle of respect for persons? The principle of community provides a basis for restricting the locations where it is sold and for restricting its public display, but not for its prohibition. If the collective decision is that persons shall not have to encounter pornography as they go about their everyday affairs, its sale and display may be restricted to places where persons will not encounter it without warning, for here we are dealing with a decision about what activities shall be done where — a coordination decision — and these decisions may be made collectively. To this extent it may even be said that the principles of legal coercion permit the enforcement of popular morality, since common moral beliefs may be what guides the collective preference. However, sale of pornography per se may not be prohibited under this principle because that would be complete prohibition of an activity violating each individual's right to decide for himself or herself whether to engage in it. Thus, the principle of community does not justify making a crime of the sale of pornography.

To determine whether the sale of pornography might be prohibitable under other principles, let us consider some of the things which may be said against pornography. It is sometimes thought to have evil effects of various kinds on people, and perhaps some of those would warrant prohibition of its sale. Among the possible effects of pornography which might be considered here are sexual arousal, changes in the kinds and frequency of sexual behavior engaged in, changes in attitudes toward sexual conduct, emotional and judgmental reactions, and increased occurrence of antisocial sex-related conduct.[5] Only a few of these, however, provide even a potential basis for prohibition under the terms of the present theory, for harmless conduct engaged in voluntarily provides no basis for legal restrictions. Thus, even if pornography causes changes in attitudes, changes in the kinds and frequency of sexual behavior, and sexual arousal, that in itself does nothing to justify its prohibition, since interference with these things is not permitted under any of the principles of legal coercion. This is true even if the sexual conduct in question may be contrary to popular morality (e.g., homosexual conduct, oral-genital relations, group sex, etc.), for there is no basis for prohibition of such conduct itself, and thus none for coercively interfering with things that lead to it. Therefore, the only alleged effect of pornography which could bring it under principles justifying its prohibition is the possibility that it causes or significantly contributes to harmful sexual conduct such as rape. Rape itself is, of course, prohibitable under the harm principle, and if rape may be prevented by prohibiting the sale of pornography, that might be sufficient to justify the interference with pornography.

The difficulty here, of course, is that of determining whether the availability of pornography does contribute to rape.[6] The U.S. Commission on Obscenity and Pornography "found no evidence to date that exposure to explicit sexual materials plays a significant role in the causation of delinquent or criminal behavior among youth or adults" and found that it "cannot conclude that exposure to erotic materials is a factor in the causation of sex crime or sex delinquency".[7] This conclusion was based mainly upon comparisons between groups of offenders (delinquent youth and sex offenders) and non-offenders with respect to their exposure to erotic materials and upon statistical studies of the relationship between the availability of these materials and the occurrence of sex crimes in Denmark and the United States. To the extent that this conclusion is correct, there is no basis for prohibition of pornography under the principles of legal coercion. However, critics of the majority on the Commission contend that significant evidence to the contrary was not given sufficent attention. Let us consider whether that evidence might alter the conclusion about prohibition of pornography.

The claim suggested by the Commission dissenters which seems to require attention is that pornography may serve to 'trigger' harmful sex crimes. The idea here is apparently that for some persons perhaps predisposed toward sexual aggression, pornography may incite sex crimes which would not occur were the exposure to pornography lacking. Evidence for this is said to be found in reports by offenders themselves who claim to have been influenced by erotic materials and in opinions of professionals such as police officials, psychiatrists and psychologists who deal with persons who commit sex offenses.[8] This evidence is not claimed to be of a highly rigorous sort, but it is claimed to deserve serious attention.

Let us suppose that what has been suggested here is true. Does it provide grounds for prohibition of the sale of pornography? The case for this would be something alone the following lines. Rape is clearly a harmful action under the terms of our respect-for-persons approach, and interference with rape is clearly permitted. Selling pornography is not in itself a harmful action since it does not deprive anyone of control to which he or she is entitled; but on the hypothesis being considered it does have a relationship with rape. This relationship is such that sometimes some persons sexually aroused by pornography commit acts of rape which they would not have committed had they not encountered the pornographic materials. Now, interference with the sale of pornography reduces its availability and, given the above relationship, may prevent some acts of rape since it may eliminate the stimulus which would trigger the offense. If pornography is easily available, those with low self-restraint are more likely to be stimulated to commit offenses which would not occur if pornography were less easy to find. Hence, the argument goes, prohibition of the sale of pornography is justifiable under the harm principle as a means to the prevention of rape.

Prohibition of the sale of pornography would certainly be an instance of an extra-inclusive legal requirement. It is not even claimed that any large proportion of those who purchase pornography are incited by it to commit rape; the claim is merely that this occasionally happens. Thus, defense of the prohibition depends upon the harm principle supplemented by the principle of necessary means, and that imposes special requirements. The prohibition must not impose major sacrifice, its burden must be fairly distributed, and it must be *necessary* to achieving the purpose. To show that it is necessary it would have to be established not only that there are cases in whch pornography triggers rape, but also that no other trigger would substitute if pornography were unavailable. There is some evidence that such a substitution would occur. It has been found that sex offenders "appear to generate their own pornography from non-sexual stimuli" and that they read "sexual meanings into images that would be devoid of erotic connotations for the normal person".[9] Noting the case of a rapist who reporting finding a housewife's description of a rape in *Ladies' Home Journal* a source of fantasy about rape, these investigators point out that "sex offenders are highly receptive to suggestions of sexual behavior congruent with their previously formed desires and will interpret the material at hand to fit their needs".[10]

The trouble is that if anything, or (so to speak) the sexiest thing available, will take the place of pornography as an incitement to rape for certain persons, the events occurrence of which we seek to prevent by banning pornography will occur anyway, and so the aim is not promoted by the prohibition, and the prohibition is not necessary to the purpose, however legitimate it may be.

There are further complications as well. One is the possibility that pornography may serve as a harmless alternative outlet for potential sex offenders.[11] If the potential rapist may sometimes satisfy his desires through pornography where he might commit rape in the absence of this alternative, an increase in rape could be the result of prohibiting sale of pornography. Another complication is the possibility that where pornographic materials appear to be an incitement to rape, their sexual aspects may be confounded with aggressive aspects. Investigators report that "stimuli expressing brutality, with or without concomitant sexual behavior, were often mentioned as disturbing, by rapists in particular. This raises the question of whether the stimulus most likely to release antisocial sexual behavior is one representing sexuality, or one representing aggression".[12] If the trigger is actually the portrayal of aggression, there would be no basis for interference with non-aggressive portrayals of sexual behavior.

These considerations indicate that even if we grant that pornography may, on occasion, have served as a stimulus to rape or other harmful sexual conduct, this is not sufficient to warrant its prohibition, for it is not sufficient to show that eliminating pornography would reduce the occurrence of these crimes. All we have in the trigger argument is something which suggests that perhaps a few specific instances of sex crimes would not occur if there were not pornography; the trigger argument does not show that the total number of such crimes could be reduced by prohibiting pornography. That is clearly not enough to say that the goal of reducing rape would be served by prohibiting sale of pornography. Consider such a claim made in a completely different area. We could point to cases in which children are injured playing on teeter-totters in playgrounds; these teeter-totter-caused injuries could be prevented if teeter-totters were banned. But there is no reason to think that this would reduce the total number of injuries to children, for they can find other ways to hurt themselves. Teeter-totters are not shown to be dangerous just because they are the locations for some injuries to children. Pornography is not shown to be dangerous simply because it may sometimes serve as a trigger to harmful acts, and this does not show that the goal of preventing harm would be served by interfering with pornography. Without more than this, prohibition of the sale of porno-graphy is a violation of the rights of persons to control their own lives.

Suppose more evidence *were* obtained, and it was demonstrated that the total number of rapes could be reduced by prohibiting the sale of porno-graphy because this would make it less likely that those who would be incited to rape would encounter the stimulus. Thus, we are supposing that it has been shown that pornography serves as a stronger stimulus to rape than the substitutes which would remain were pornography eliminated, that its 'trigger' effect is more significant than its 'cathartic' effect, and so on. Then it could be claimed that by denying pornography to these rape-prone persons we are promoting the legitimate goal of preventing harm. Very well, but *even then* there would be no justification for a complete prohibition on the sale of pornography. Suppose those who wish to have pornography and who are not incited to harmful conduct by it, form private 'pornograhy clubs', membership in which is limited to those who show they can use pornography safely. The idea seems a bit ludicrous, but its possibility shows that complete prohibition is not necessary to preventing the rape-prone from being incited by pornography, and so such prohibition would not be permitted under the principle of necessary means.

It might be noted that despite the fact that the dissenting members of the U.S. Commission on Obscenity and Pornography pointed so insistently to the possibility that pornography triggers sex crimes, they claim that it is not necessary to establish such a relationship in order to justify the prohibition of pornography. "The government interest in regulating pornography has always related primarily to the prevention of moral corruption and *not* to prevention of overt criminal acts and conduct ... . The basic question is whether and to what extent society may establish and maintain certain moral standards." [13] Put this way, the case against pornography is entirely based on a belief in the enforcement of popular morality. Beyond what is allowed under the principle of community, there is no basis for the enforcement of popular morality on any view which purports to respect the moral importance of persons. Thus, unless the facts about pornography turn out to be vastly different from what they appear to be, its prohibition remains a violation of the principle of respect for persons.

10.4. THE PROBLEM OF OFFENSIVE CONDUCT

Is it justifiable to use coercive law to interfere with *offensive* conduct? Among the possible restrictions discussed under this heading are prohibitions of public nudity, of conduct which causes noise or unpleasant odors, of vulgar language, and of conduct which indicates a lack of respect for members of specific groups.[14] Evaluation of this type of legislation of course depends upon whether it can be brought under some acceptable inclusionary principle. One possibility is that this type of legislation should be the subject of a distinct inclusionary principle, *the offense principle.* The offense principle would authorize prohibition of conduct offensive to others, at least when certain conditions are satisfied. Let us first consider this approach to the problem of offensive conduct.

In favor of some sort of offense principle is the fact that some legislation apparently lacking any other basis is relatively uncontroversial. There is, for example, little dispute in contemporary America about whether nudity should be permitted just anywhere where someone feels like going nude, even less dispute about whether sexual intercourse or defecation should be permitted just anywhere. Even Mill saw no reason to object to this kind of legislation, saying of 'offenses against decency' that they are "a violation of good manners and, coming thus within the category of offenses against others, may rightly be prohibited".[15] Pulling in the other direction is the fact that it is difficult to see how a principle could be formulated that would allow for prohibition of these kinds of conduct without also permitting prohibition of virtually anything that happens to be widely disliked, or even disliked by a minority. If nudity may be prohibited because people are offended by it, then why not the wearing of strange hairstyles, or dirty clothing, the drinking of disapproved beverages, demonstrations of affection between persons of different races or of the same sex? If conduct may be prohibited merely because someone feels offended by it, very little could be said against most uses of legal coercion.

Plausible attempts to permit some prohibition of offensive conduct have been developed, however, and we may proceed by giving them some attention. Joel Feinberg has proposed that an offense principle might be acceptable provided that it is carefully limited.[16] As one limitation, he suggests the "standard of universality", which allows offensiveness to warrant coercion only when the feeling of offense "could reasonably be expected from almost any person chosen at random, taking the nation as a whole, and not because the individual selected belongs to some faction, clique, or party".[17] He finds, however, that this standard itself must be qualified so as to permit coercion for offensive conduct "that consists in the flaunting of abusive, mocking, insulting behavior of a sort bound to upset, alarm, or irritate those it insults, . . . even though the behavior would *not* offend the entire population".[18] This qualified version of Feinberg's standard of universality has been usefully stated by Donald VanDeVeer as requiring that the conduct in question "either (1) offend almost anyone chosen at random, or (2) so seriously ridicule certain persons that it is bound to anger and irritate them".[19]

Condition (1) is designed to preclude use of the offense principle when only limited groups within the society find conduct offensive, as the racially prejudiced would find the conduct of a racially mixed couple walking hand-in-hand, or as those with eccentric susceptibilities might find virtually any conduct; condition (2) is designed to except from the first condition the case of offensive attacks on specific sub-groups of a population, such as ridicule of specific racial groups which might not offend anyone chosen at random.[20]

As a further condition on the offense principle, Feinberg puts forth the "standard of reasonable avoidability", which disallows use of the offense principle to warrant prohibition of conduct the offensiveness of which is avoidable "easily and effectively . . . with no unreasonable effort or inconvenience".[21] This standard would not allow the offense principle to apply to the selling of pornography in a privately-owned store (one may easily avoid being offended by not going in), but would allow it to apply to placing pornographic billboards on public thoroughfares (one would have to go out of one's way to avoid that).

Finally, Feinberg would permit the offense principle to be used only if it is qualified further so that "the person constrained by the law from being offensive to others must be granted an allowable alternative outlet or mode of expression".[22] It is unclear just what this condition entails, however, for Feinberg offers no general account of the concept of an alternative outlet.

Perhaps the major concern about Feinberg's offense principle is that it may permit coercion too easily. Even with Feinberg's conditions, virtually any conduct which occurs in public and which is widely thought offensive, may be prohibited. What a person does on Main Street in full view of whoever happens to be there is not protected by the standard of reasonable avoidability nor by the alternative outlets condition; anything done in such a location may be prohibitable provided that enough people are offended by it. Feinberg argues that conduct is offensive when it causes various "unpleasant states [such as] irritating sensations (e.g., bad smells and loud noises); unaffected disgust and acute repugnance as caused, for example, by extreme vulgarity and filth; shocked moral, religious, or patriotic sensibilities;

unsettling anger or irritation as caused by another's 'obnoxious, insulting, rude, or insolent behavior'; and shameful embarrassment or invaded privacy, as caused, for example, by another's nudity or indecency".[23] It hardly seems necessary to point out that human beings are capable of having these feelings about virtually anything.

Two aspects of Feinberg's discussion might be thought to answer this objection. One is the way in which he allows competing interests to weigh against the interest in not being offended before any prohibition is fully justified. One reason why the appearance in public in a racist community of an interracial couple cannot be prohibited, he suggests, is that the couple's interests in free association and movement outweigh the competing interests in not being offended.[24] This move, however, can work only where special interests are involved; it cannot protect actions in which the agent has no significant stake. If even actions of no particular importance to the agent could be protected in this way, the offense principle would be vacuous, since offensiveness would then always lack sufficient weight to warrant interference with action. Yet it is not clear that even actions of no particular importance to the agent should not be protected from interference on grounds of mere offense.

A second aspect of Feinberg's discussion addresses this problem more directly. He acknowledges that his view appears susceptible to the charge that it would permit prohibition of quite innocent activities in hypothetical cases in which those activities affect others in the way that actually offensive conduct (thus prohibitable under the offense principle) affects some. What if, for instance, eating chocolate affected onlookers in the same way that eating excrement affects them? To this Feinberg responds that if "the sight of a person eating chocolate affects all onlookers in [some hypothetical] society in *precisely the same way* as the sight of a person eating excrement affects all onlookers in our society, then why should one want the hypothetical law to treat that hypothetical case any differently from the way in which the actual law treats the actual case?"[25] The trouble with this reply is that the offense principle is not so restrictive as the example suggests; under the offense principle the innocent activity need only affect onlookers in the same way as only mildly offensive activities affect others. Reportedly some persons are embarrassed by the appearance on television of advertisements for condoms and for feminine hygiene products such as tampons and douches. The offense principle thus would permit prohibition of conduct which affected virtually everyone in the way those ads affect some; if wearing white socks caused this kind of embarrassment, it would be prohibitable.

Further, any other activity which had a similar affect on people generally would also be prohibitable. The point to emphasize is that this means that any action which causes general displeasure is subject to prohibition. This is because there is no apparent basis for allowing some displeasures to count for prohibition while not allowing other displeasures. Hence, the offense principle says that the fact that something is widely disliked is a good reason for its prohibition.

Can the principle of respect for persons permit displeasure at an activity, even widely shared displeasure, to count as a good reason for prohibition of an activity? From the respect-for-persons perspective, the question is that of to whom the decision as to whether a person shall engage in an activity which will cause widespread (but possibly quite temporary) displeasure should be assigned. Does the person have the right to make this decision unilaterally, or do those who would be caused the displeasure have the right to make or participate in the decision? Which assignment of control best reflects the commitment to the importance of each person's having control over his or her own life? That this sort of decision is properly made by the individual unilaterally seems quite clear. This may be seen both through an abstract argument and through an argument from example.

The abstract argument is based upon consideration of the kind of liberty of action which would remain if others' mere displeasure at one's actions were sufficient to give them the right to decide whether one may engage in the action. To remain true to its tradition, respect-for-persons ethics must include the view that persons' rights to choose their own actions set limits on the rights of others to control them. If others' mere displeasure were sufficient ground for interference, one's right to choose actions for oneself would be so insubstantial as to be virtually meaningless; one would then have the right to select unilaterally one's actions only if others chose not to protest against the selections. This would mean that others lack the right to interfere only if they do not really want it. This is not a standard which sets meaningful limits on others' rights to interfere in one's actions.

The argument from example will make this problem more concrete. Suppose we have a person who is widely known and admired for his accomplishments in some sphere, say, someone like Muhammad Ali. Ali was, let us agree, the best boxer in history. He is now perhaps well past his prime, yet periodically he announces his intention to make a comeback. Many observers, however, apparently felt that Ali would be embarrassingly unsuccessful in a comeback attempt, and would have preferred to remember him as he was at his peak. In short, Ali's comeback attempts caused widespread distress among fans of the Ali legend. Yet surely Ali himself is the only one who has the right to decide whether he shall attempt another come-back. How could a view which assigns primary importance to persons' rights to control their own lives say differently? But this is an action which would cause others a kind of unavoidable mental distress apparently not distin-guishable in principle from that meant to be covered by the offense principle. Further, the view that Ali should be allowed to make his own decision does not seem to depend on how important the attempt would be to Ali; it should be his decision even if it is not of great importance to him. Thus, others' mere displeasure at one's actions does not give them the right to interfere, and the offense principle must be rejected by respect-for-persons ethics.

An alternative to Feinberg's offense principle is proposed by Donald VanDeVeer. He calls his version of the offense principle "the Standard of Reasonable Restraint". This standard (subject to competing considerations) allows legal coercion to protect individuals from "those who maliciously, recklessly, or negligently disregard their interest in not being harmed by seriously offensive actions".[26]

Thusly stated, it can hardly be objectionable to anyone who accepts the harm principle. At least one cannot object that it is too permissive, since it permits interference only when the offensive conduct threatens harm; that would be permitted by the harm principle itself. Nonetheless, the principle raises some questions. Why is the mental element required, when surely someone who is being *harmed* by another's non-negligent, unintentional, but seriously offensive conduct has some claim to justifiable interference? Further, since VanDeVeer claims[27] that there is always some harm involved in being offended, the reference to both harm and offense in his statement of the standard seems redundant. If the redundancy is eliminated, the standard says that the sort of conduct which gives rise to justifiable coercive action is conduct which is seriously offensive. Little, however, is offered to help identify *seriously offensive* conduct. If seriously offensive conduct is that which causes the kind of harm prohibitable under the harm principle, then the standard is unobjectionable, but adds little to the harm principle. If seriously offensive conduct does not necessarily cause the sort of harm which comes under the harm principle, then this standard is subject to the same objections as the Feinberg proposals.

If we assume that VanDeVeer intends his offense principle to be an elaboration of the implications of the harm principle, he is following the proposal of Bayles that the best way to handle offensive conduct is through an extension of the harm principle rather than through an independent offense principle. Bayles suggests that the "interest in not being offended may be divided into more specific interests depending upon the sensibility affronted and the object causing the offense . . . . Each such interest can then be evaluated as providing a good reason for criminal legislation".[28] The basis for evaluating the various interests is to be the perspective of the reasonable man. If sensibilities "are to provide a good reason for prohibiting conduct, they must be such as a reasonable man might have".[29] Unfortunately, both Feinberg and VanDeVeer have convincing objections to this last step of Bayles. Feinberg points out that "many of the forms of offense discussed . . . seem to have nothing to do with reasonableness. It is neither reasonable nor unreasonable but simply 'non-reasonable' to be bothered by the sight of nude bodies, public defecation, disgusting 'food', and the like".[30] VanDe-Veer argues that those with abnormal or eccentric sensibilities do have a claim to restraint because of them. If someone will be genuinely harmed through being offended because of an irrational belief, should this not be protected?[31]

The possibility of extending the harm principle to cover some cases of offense, however, warrants consideration from the respect-for-persons perspective. A person is harmed, on this view, when his or her personal sphere is invaded. Some problematic cases of offensive conduct could come under this description. When offensive conduct results in something more serious than mere displeasure, something approaching what we might call psychological harm, it could qualify as an unacceptable interference in someone's mentation.[32] Since some seriouly offensive conduct may be brought under the harm principle, the need for the offense principle as an independent principle is unclear.

When the need for an offense principle is questioned, Feinberg has an initially convincing answer. He describes an example of a piece of conduct which apparently would be prohibitable only under an offense principle, but which will widely be thought properly subjected to interference. The example is worth quoting in full:

Consider then the man who walks down the main street of a town at mid-day. In the middle of a block in the central part of town, he stops, opens his briefcase, and pulls out a portable folding camp-toilet. In the prescribed manner, he attaches a plastic bag to its under side, sets it on the sidewalk, and proceeds to defecate in it, to the utter amazement and disgust of the passers-by. While he is thus relieving himself, he unfolds a large banner which reads "This is what I think of the Ruritanians" (substitute "Niggers", "Kikes", "Spics", "Dagos", "Polacks", or "Hunkies"). Another placard placed prominently next to him invites ladies to join him in some of the more bizarre sexual-excretory perversions mentioned in Kraft-Ebbing [sic] and includes a large-scale graphic painting of the conduct he solicits. For those who avert their eyes too quickly, he plays an obscene phonograph record on a small portable machine, and accompanies its raunchier parts with grotesquely lewd bodily motions. He concludes his public performance by tasting some of his own excrement, and after savouring it slowly and thoroughly in the manner of a true epicure, he consumes it. He then dresses, ties the plastic bag containing the rest of the excrement, places it carefully in his briefcase, and continues on his way.[33]

There is no apparent reason to claim that the offense caused by this man constitutes harm of a sort which would warrant interference under the harm principle. Yet most find the example convincing in that they believe that it ought to be possible to put a stop to this sort of conduct. Recognition of an offense principle would accommodate that view. However, in view of the foregoing objections to the offense principle, that remains an unattractive approach. I propose that, instead of adopting an offense principle on a par with other principles of legal coercion, we consider whether cases such as this one might be brought under one of the principles already established as part of the present theory. I shall suggest that limited interference can be authorized through the principle of community, provided that its various conditions are satisfied.

The first question concerning the application of the principle of community to the Feinberg example is whether it involves an other-regarding common-decision. The decision type that it seems to involve is a coordination decision. These, again, are decisions that certain areas be used for designated activities and not for activities incompatible with the designated ones. The performance Feinberg describes would presumably be found so distracting as to make carrying on the various activities ordinarily performed on public streets quite difficult. As an activity which thus disrupts the activities for which most public places are normally used, it may be restricted under the principle of community.

The principle of community allows for the important safeguards that Feinberg applies to the offense principle. The alternative outlets requirement is provided for in the similar condition on the principle of community. It means that activities can be restricted only as to time and place, and so only activities for which references to time and place are part of their descriptions (e.g., going nude wherever and whenever one wants to) can be completely prohibited (e.g., nudity cannot be prohibited everywhere). Feinberg's reasonable avoidability requirement is also supported in that prohibition of offensive conduct under the principle of community involves coordination decisions. That is, the decision to prohibit specified conduct in specified locations qualifies as an other-regarding common-decision when it is a coordination decision, and it qualifies as a coordination decision only if it concerns activities incompatible with ones designated for the location. Offensive conduct which is reasonably avoidable is not incompatible with other activities, and thus does not qualify for prohibition under the principle of community.

The principle of community does not incorporate Feinberg's standard of universality, however. As we saw earlier, Feinberg himself found reason to limit it.[34] While its provisions are not derivable from the principle of community, the present view does contain features which may accommodate the motivations for it. Since the principle of community refers to collective preference, it will be inapplicable where the feeling of offense is not widely shared. As for verbal abuse of individuals which is not offensive to the population in general, the more extreme forms of such conduct could fall under the harm principle.

The principle of community is more restrictive of interferences with offensive conduct than is the offense principle in two ways. First, the former principle allows interference only with other-regarding common-decisions, and not with person-decisions such as Ali's decision whether to attempt another comeback. Second, only relatively serious kinds of offense would qualify for interference under the principle of community, since only relatively serious kinds would be sufficiently disruptive of other activities to generate a need for a coordination decision. The offense principle does not seem to distinguish degrees of offensiveness as conditions on interference.

In some respect, of course, this application of the principle of community is open to objections similar to some brought against the offense principle. Despite constraints contained in the principle of community, it is still possible for a collective to impose some restrictions based on little more than its own strong preferences. Take, for instance, the case of an American reporter in Iran who caused outrage among Iranians who observed him running in shorts; it seems his bare legs violated the Islamic code of modesty. The principle of community could permit some restrictions along these lines, since a decision as to where persons shall go bare-legged could be a coordination decision, given attitudes toward that conduct similar to American attitudes toward public nudity. There is of course no basis for total prohibition here, but the idea that even restrictions of time and place can be imposed on these grounds may still seem unattractive.

Despite sharing these reservations, I believe we have sufficient reason to give them up. Feinberg's example and others of its kind are persuasive in indicating the need for some restrictions in this area. The derivation of the principle of community from the principle of respect for persons explains how those sentiments can be reconciled with basic ethical concerns and provides a theoretical rationale for the restrictions. These arguments for the restrictions, plus a recognition of the aforementioned limits on the application of the principle of community in this area, combine with three further considerations to make this case.

First, the fact that some restrictions based upon feelings of offense are permitted by the principle of community does not mean that such prohibitions must not be criticized. They do not necessarily violate the principle of respect for persons, but they are properly subject to criticism when they are based on foolish, irrational, superstitious, or otherwise objectionable values or beliefs. What is appropriately criticized is not the right of the collective to exercise its preference concerning where certain activities shall be performed, but the preferences themselves and the beliefs and values on which they are based. Thus, in the Iranian case, what is appropriately criticized is the foolishness of the view that there is something seriously wrong with appearing in public with bare legs. Or, to take a case from American culture, if a reformer wishes to change American laws requiring women to cover their breasts in public, the belief that there is something wrong with not covering the breasts is the appropriate object of criticism – unless, of course, bare-breastedness is prohibited everywhere. In short, foolish views should still be condemned as foolish even if it is not necessarily a violation of respect for persons to base some restrictions on them.[35]

A second consideration is the fact that no serious punishment could be justifiable for offenses of this kind. We saw in Section 9.5 that there are two upper bounds on the severity of punishment, and the application of both of them to this case indicates that no severe punishment could be justified. The proportionality requirement would permit no severe punishment, for the offenses in question involve no harm to persons (if they did involve harm, they would be punishable under the harm principle). All that is threatened by illegal offensive conduct is one quite limited dimension of collective control over the common. Such offenses could only be found quite insignificant. Further, the boundary set by the need for deterrence would also be likely to be quite low. Perhaps because there is seldom anything to be gained by offending people at random, there is no indication that the number of such offenses would increase significantly if they were not illegal. Informal social pressure usually seems to be sufficient to deter offensive conduct, so it is difficult to imagine that anything beyond very light penalties could be required on deterrence grounds. In view of these considerations, the possibility of outlawing some offensive conduct under the principle of community hardly seems worrisome. Surely concern about prohibition of offensive conduct in the past has often been partly the result of the use of overly severe penalties for very minor offenses.

Finally, consider how another of the worries arising from Feinberg's offense principle applies to the present view. There was the concern that the offense principle might authorize prohibition of the public appearance of an interracial couple in a racist community. The same concern can be raised about handling offensive conduct under the principle of community. I shall argue that Feinberg's answer to this objection is sound when placed in the context of the present theory. His answer, again, was that the couple's interests in free association and movement outweigh the competing interests in not being offended. Now if a case for an interest in free association and movement can be grounded in the principle of respect for persons (as seems likely), then we would have the basis for a special exclusionary principle precluding laws which fail to respect that special interest. The point would be not that the community lacks sufficient justification for the use of *coercion*, but that it lacks sufficient justification for use of this special *form* of coercion. Thus, this prohibition could be ruled out despite being supported by the principle of community. Further, when placed in this context, the competing interests solution is not open to the objection that insignificant interests are not protected. Such interests are protected by the primary exclusionary principle, and since the principle of community authorizes intervention only when relatively serious offensiveness is involved, insignificant interests are protected from undue interference as well.

10.5. CONCLUDING REMARKS

The application of the theoretical framework developed here will occasionally require two kinds of additional investigation. One of them is empirical. Empirical investigation can play a role in the application of several of the principles of legal coercion. For example, we may discover empirically the hazardous nature of some practice previously thought to be harmless or the extent of the costs involved in providing a certain sort of assistance. This information, in conjunction with the relevant principles, will yield judgments about the permissibility of various kinds of legislation. Further, once it has been determined that a type of legislation does not violate the principle of respect for persons, empirical concerns remain relevant to the overall assessment of legislation, since, of course, some morally permissible kinds of laws may be too costly or inefficient. I take it to be a virtue of the theory that it makes a significant place for sociological, economic, and other kinds of empirical study. Utilitarian views have always done this, but Kantian approaches sometimes seem to imply the complete irrelevance of facts and inquiries of obvious importance. If the present theory succeeds in defining a plausible role for such matters, it will perhaps serve as an alternative framework for those who have adopted utilitarianism because no other view seemed to recognize the importance of empirical investigation.

The other kind of additional investigation which will be required for some applications is philosophical. This is a recognition of a fact perhaps best learned from the law, viz, that the application of principles to cases is not a merely mechanical drawing out of implications from premises complete in themselves, but often requires creative argument and interpretation. Handling some issues within the framework developed here will sometimes depend upon further conceptual and justificatory work. To decide, for instance, how the law should deal with fetuses would require consideration of the question of whether fetuses are persons; to decide whether the law should be used to encourage reverse discrimination would require inquiry into the exclusionary principle dealing with discrimination. General principles cannot contain within themselves clearcut answers to every case. Thus, the general theory is enriched through discussion of more particular cases, and can be made truly complete only through discussion of all the issues to which it would apply. On the other hand, discussions of particular cases and issues are never shown to be fully satisfactory until the general framework of which they are a part is articulated and examined. This work, of course, has been given over primarily to the latter task, although it is hoped that enough has been said about applications to make the framework of principles useful in the handling of various specific issues.

Finally, something might be said about just what sort of view it is that has been defended here. While I am not fond of labels — because they tend to be misleading and often get in the way of seeing what is actually being said — their use seems inevitable. Thus, I would call this a 'civil libertarian' view, meaning by that a view which recognizes secondary exclusionary principles and inclusionary principles which are, so to speak, no more inclusionary than those accepted here. Civil libertarianism may be contrasted with legal moralism on the one hand, and economic libertarianism on the other. The legal moralist supports additional inclusionary principles permitting the enforcement of popular morality, or of critical morality without regard for the stringency of the requirements enforced. Such a view also typically accepts stronger forms of paternalism and weaker exclusionary principles (if any). The economic libertarian would reject the welfare principle and the principle of community, often on the ground that these principles permit people to be treated as mere means. The principal mistake of the moralist is the failure to recognize that morality itself sets limits to the use of coercion even for good aims, while the central error of the economic libertarian is the failure to recognize that the requirement that persons not be treated as mere means is itself based on the positive requirement that they must be treated as ends in themselves.

NOTES

INTRODUCTION

[1] Noel B. Reynolds, 'The Enforcement of Morals and the Rule of Law', *Georgia Law Reivew* 11 (September, 1977), p. 1325.

[2] I refer to theories which take as their fundamental commitment a concern for the moral importance of persons by the term 'respect for persons'. The works I have in mind here include John Rawls, *A Theory of Justice* (Cambridge, Mass.: Harvard University Press, 1971); Robert Nozick, *Anarchy, State, and Utopia* (New York: Basic Books, 1974); and Ronald Dworkin, *Taking Rights Seriously* (Cambridge, Mass.: Harvard University Press, 1977). I have developed some specific criticisms of Nozick and Dworkin, respectively, in 'Nozick, Libertarianism, and Rights', *Arizona Law Review* 19 (1977), pp. 212–227; and in a review of *Taking Rights Seriously* in *Vanderbilt Law Review* 31 (March, 1978), pp. 450–471.

[3] For more extensive discussions of methods in ethics which are generally compatible with the approach adopted here, see Rawls' comments on what he calls 'reflective equilibrium' in *A Theory of Justice*, and R. M. Hare's *Freedom and Reason* (London: Oxford University Press, 1963).

[4] See Vinit Haksar, 'Coercive Proposals', *Political Theory* 4 (February, 1976), pp. 65–79.

[5] Here I leave aside some important and difficult questions about the full analysis of the concept of coercion. Since my concern is with the justification of uses of coercion uncontroversially accepted as such, resolution of these issues is not critical here. For further discussion of the concept of coercion, see, e.g., Robert Nozick, 'Coercion', in *Philosophy, Politics, and Society*, 4th Series, eds. P. Laslett *et al.* (Oxford: Blackwell, 1972); and *Coercion*, Nomos XIV, eds. J. Chapman and J. R. Pennock (Chicago: Aldine, 1972).

CHAPTER ONE

[1] *Foundations of the Metaphysics of Morals*, trans. L. W. Beck (Indianapolis: Bobbs-Merrill), p. 47.

[2] *Ibid.*, p. 48.

[3] E.g., on the Rawlsian model, the point would be that parties in the original position would choose to have their choices in real life respected except when contrary to principles adopted in the original position.

[4] I have previously made use of the idea of the unencumbered will in my article, 'The Principle of Paternalism', *American Philosophical Quarterly* 14 (January, 1977), pp. 61–69.

[5] The reference to one's life being under one's own control may ruffle some deterministic feathers. If human behavior is causally determined by environmental or genetic factors or some combination of those, it may be questioned whether anyone has willful

control over his or her own actions. However, what is intended by that expression is, I think, not particularly controversial and is not threatened by the possible truth of deterministic accounts of human behavior. As the expression is used here, one has willful control over one's own body so long as its movement and lack of movement are not inconsistent with what one chooses to do, and are not brought about by the choices of others in a way which makes it impossible for one to choose otherwise or to act otherwise if one were to choose to do so. The choices involved here may be understood simply as those phenomena commonly described as such; no assumptions need be made as to the metaphysical status of these choices nor as to their further causal determinants.

6 See, e.g., Elizabeth V. Spelman, 'On Treating Persons as Persons', *Ethics* 88 (January, 1978), pp. 150–161.

CHAPTER TWO

1 *On Liberty*, Ch. 1.
2 *The Enforcement of Morals* (London: Oxford University Press, 1965).
3 For a summary of the views of several critics who attack Mill in this way, see Section II of J. C. Rees, 'A Re-Reading of Mill on Liberty', in *Limits of Liberty*, ed. P. Radcliff (Belmont, Ca.: Wadsworth Publishing Co., 1966).
4 *Liberty, Equality, Fraternity*, Preface to the Second Edition, 1874.
5 Martin Golding, *Philosophy of Law* (Englewood Cliffs: Prentice-Hall, 1975), p. 57.
6 Ernest Nagel, 'The Enforcement of Morals', in *Ethics and Public Policy*, ed. Tom L. Beauchamp (Englewood Cliffs: Prentice-Hall, 1975), p. 265.
7 *Ibid.*, p. 268.
8 *The Enforcement of Morals*, p. 102.
9 My treatment of these matters follows in some respects those of Michael Bayles and Dudley Knowles. I argue, however, that their attempts to avoid the problems of defining a protected sphere are not successful. For their treatments, see Michael Bayles, 'Legislating Morality', *Wayne Law Review* 22 (March, 1976), pp. 759–762; Dudley R. Knowles, 'A Reformulation of the Harm Principle', *Political Theory* 6 (May, 1978), pp. 233–246.
10 An 'action token' is a particular instance of an action having a certain generic description, while the description indicates an 'action type'. Thus, if, in a baseball game, two successive batters hit home runs, we have two tokens of the action type 'hitting a home run"
11 This is Bayles' position. See *ibid.*, pp. 761–762.
12 For Devlin's views, see especially 'Morals and the Criminal Law', in *The Enforcement of Morals*. Devlin's position is criticized by H. L. A. Hart in *Law, Liberty, and Morality* (Stanford: Stanford University Press, 1963) and in 'Social Solidarity and the Enforcement of Morality', *University of Chicago Law Review* 35 (1967).
13 Cf. Bayles, 'Legislating Morality', pp. 760–761.
14 Knowles, 'Reformulation', p. 238.
15 This is Knowles' proposal. See *ibid.*, esp. Section II.
16 See *ibid.*, pp. 244–245.
17 *The Enforcement of Morals*, pp. 16–17.
18 ' "Harmless Immoralities" and Offensive Nuisances' in *Issues in Law and Morality*, eds. N. Care and T. Trelogan (Cleveland: Case Western Reserve Press, 1973), p. 95.

[19] 'Law, Liberty, and Indecency', in *Philosophical Issues in Law*, ed. K. Kipnis (Englewood Cliffs: Prentice-Hall, 1977), p. 86. Originally published in *Philosophy* 49 (April, 1974).

[20] 'Legislating Morality', p. 762.

[21] Cf. R. Sartorius: "If one sincerely believes that the performance of a certain kind of act is wrong, what better reason could he have for seeking . . . to prevent it?" ('The Enforcement of Morality', *Yale Law Journal* 81 [April, 1972], p. 894.) See also A. R. Louch: "Now there is something compelling about the move from the charge of gross immorality to punishment. The legal moralist seems to be on strong ground in claiming that murder is punishable because wrong, and therefore that anything that is wrong, is punishable". ('Sins and Crimes', in *Morality and the Law*, ed. Richard Wasserstrom [Belmont: Wadsworth Publishing Co., 1971], p. 74.)

[22] See Hart, *Law, Liberty, and Morality*, pp. 17–24. See also Ronald Dworkin, 'Lord Devlin and the Enforcement of Morals', in Wasserstrom, *Morality and the Law*, pp. 61–67.

[23] See Sartorius, 'The Enforcement of Morality', pp. 892–898. Cf. Bayles, 'Legislating Morality', pp. 762–767.

[24] This interpretation is really only a particular instance of the view discussed in Section 2.2 according to which the debate is over what purposes law should serve.

[25] See generally, Louch, 'Sins And Crimes'.

[26] See Devlin, 'Democracy and Morality', in *The Enforcement of Morals*.

[27] Devlin, *The Enforcement of Morals*, p. 17.

[28] See Graham Hughes, 'Morals and the Criminal Law', *Yale Law Journal* 71 (1962), p. 662; also Dworkin, 'Lord Devlin and the Enforcement of Morals'.

[29] 'Legislating Morality', p. 764.

[30] Another instance in which the failure to make this distinction leads to problems is in the differences between Devlin and Dworkin. For more on this see my review of *Taking Rights Seriously*, pp. 451–455.

[31] Cf. Mill: "To have a right, then, is, I conceive, to have something which society ought to defend me in the possession of". (*Utilitarianism*, Ch. V, Par. 25.) See also H. L. A. Hart, 'Are There Any Natural Rights?' *Philosophical Review* 64 (1955), Section I(A). Rights may be *positive* or *negative*. Negative rights are rights that certain actions *not be* performed, while positive rights are rights that certain actions *be* performed. See Chapter Five.

[32] *Philosophy of Law*, p. 58.

[33] 'Victimless Crimes', *Ethics* 87 (1977), p. 307.

CHAPTER THREE

[1] See, e.g., Joel Feinberg, *Social Philosophy* (Englewood Cliffs: Prentice-Hall, 1973), p. 26; Feinberg, 'Harm and Self-Interest', in *Law, Morality, and Society*, eds. P. M. S. Hacker and J. Raz (Oxford: Clarendon Press, 1977), p. 285; Hyman Gross, *A Theory of Criminal Justice* (New York: Oxford University Press, 1979), pp. 115–119; and Michael Bayles, *Principles of Legislation*, Detroit: Wayne State University Press, 1978), Ch. V.

[2] Cf. Gross, *A Theory of Criminal Justice*, pp. 115–117.

[3] Feinberg, *Social Philosophy*, p. 26.

[4] Feinberg, 'Harm and Self-Interest'.

5 Bayles, *Principles of Legislation*, p. 97.
6 *Ibid.*, p. 100.
7 *Ibid.*, p. 104.
8 *Ibid.*, p. 105.
9 *Ibid.*, p. 107.
10 John Kleinig, 'Crime and the Concept of Harm', *American Philosophical Quarterly* 15 (January, 1978), p. 33.
11 *Ibid.*, p. 31.
12 Cf. Michael H. Shapiro, 'Legislating the Control of Behavior Control: Autonomy and the Coercive Use of Organic Therapies', *Southern California Law Review* 47 (1974), p. 246n.
13 Of course, there are many difficult questions suggested by this classification; however, since these problems affect the theory of the proper uses of law only with respect to its application to certain kinds of cases, I shall not here attempt to do more with these issues.
14 See below, Ch. 6.
15 *Ibid.*
16 Cf. Feinberg, *Social Philosophy*, p. 27.
17 Cf. Joel Feinberg, 'Legal Paternalism', *Canadian Journal of Philosophy* 1 (1971), pp. 106–109; Bayles, *Principles of Legislation*, p. 105.

CHAPTER FOUR

1 This definition of paternalism is roughly equivalent to that of Gerald Dworkin in 'Paternalism', except that it incorporates the view of Gert and Culver that paternalism sometimes involves wrongs (e.g., lying) other than interference with liberty of action. (See Bernard Gert and Charles Culver, 'Paternalistic Behavior', *Philosophy and Public Affairs* 6 [Fall, 1976].) I have not adopted the further conditions proposed by Gert and Culver because they seem to me to restrict unduly the class of paternalistic actions. Their denial that one can act paternalistically with respect to infants strays too far from the original meaning of the term. Moreover, the same moral issue arises (i.e., is the intervention justified?) whenever one intervenes in the life of a person for the person's own good, regardless of whether the person believes himself to be competent, regardless of whether the person will immediately consent, and regardless of whether the person is acting in a fully voluntary manner. To treat those factors as requiring separate classifications needlessly multiplies the number of situation-types that must be considered. For similar reasons, I have also not adopted the view of Tom Beauchamp that 'paternalism' refers only to interferences with voluntary actions. (See 'Paternalism and Biobehavioral Control', *The Monist* 60 [January, 1977], pp. 62–80.)
2 See Jeffrie G. Murphy, 'Incompetence and Paternalism', *Archiv für Rechts und Sozialphilosophie* 60 (1974), pp. 465–486.
3 'Paternalism and Morality', *Ratio* 13 (June, 1971), p. 62.
4 Cf. Murphy, 'Incompetence and Paternalism',
5 Stated in this way, the principle of paternalism is applicable to paternalistic *coercion*, but not necessarily to paternalistic actions which may not be, strictly speaking, coercive. Paternalistic lying (e.g., the doctor who tells her dying patient that everything will be

fine) may be a case of this. While I think the same general approach is applicable to non-coercive paternalism, the principle would have to be stated somewhat differently to apply to that. I do not restate it here because the present concern *is* with coercion.

[6] Mass., 370 N.E. 2d 417.

[7] *Ibid.*, p. 423.

[8] *Ibid.*, p. 429.

[9] *Ibid.*, p. 428.

[10] *Ibid.*, p. 430.

[11] One would, of course, like to be able to say something stronger than that this conclusion "seems reasonable"; there is, however, no reason to suppose that there will always be available evidence sufficient to warrant stronger conclusions.

[12] This is the way the case of one Jehovah's Witness is made to appear by the court in *Application of the President and Directors of Georgetown College, Inc.*, 118 U.S. App. D.C. 80, 331 F. 2d 1000, cert. denied, 377 U.S. 978, 84 S. Ct. 1883, 12 L.Ed. 2d 746 (1964).

CHAPTER FIVE

[1] Cf. Nozick, *Anarchy, State, and Utopia*, p. 57.

[2] Kant's own view on this issue is admittedly somewhat ambiguous; however, there is reason to think that he would not make the duty to aid others completely optional. See, e.g., Charles Fried, *Right and Wrong* (Cambridge: Harvard University Press, 1978), pp. 115–116; also Jeffrie G. Murphy, *Kant: The Philosophy of Right* (London: Macmillan, 1970), pp. 144–146.

[3] The dimensions of this limitation are explored more fully in Section 5.4. below.

[4] Variants of this view may be found in John Kleinig, 'Good Samaritanism', *Philosophy and Public Affairs* 5 (1976), pp. 382–407; and in Bruce Russell, 'On the Relative Strictness of Negative and Positive Duties', *American Philosophical Quarterly* 14 (April, 1977), pp. 87–97.

[5] For a description of this case, see Louis Waller, 'Rescue and the Common Law: England and Australia' in *The Good Samaritan and the Law*, ed. J. Ratcliffe (Garden City: Anchor Books, 1966), pp. 142–143.

[6] Herbert Fingarette describes such a case in 'Some Moral Aspects of Good Samaritanship', in *The Good Samaritan and the Law*, pp. 213–214.

[7] The problem here is, of course, similar to that of choosing a strategy for decision under uncertainty. The conservative attitude toward risk is represented by the maximin strategy, which calls for choosing the alternative, which has the best worst outcome. If the maximin strategy is supportable, then there might be a case for required assistance in circumstances like those of the present case. However, even Rawls, who argues for the adoption of the maximin strategy under the special circumstances of his original position, does not claim that the strategy is best for all circumstances. (See Rawls, *A Theory of Justice*, Section 26.)

[8] For more on this, see Section 10.2.

CHAPTER SIX

[1] This example is adapted from Bayles, *Principles of Legislation*, p. 158.

2 Without dwelling on the issue, I shall assume that some form of democracy is the method for collective decision-making which would be required by the principle of respect for persons; of course, I have not demonstrated that this is so.

3 Assuming that animals are not persons.

4 Here I assume that there is no significant scarcity of apples. Scarcity situations are discussed shortly as 'elimination decisions'.

5 The label 'other-regarding' is of course taken from Mill's *On Liberty*. The decisions so labeled differ from their counterparts in Mill primarily in being limited to decisions about the common and in being defined so as not to include every decision which merely affects others. John Locke may have had something similar to the position I am taking in mind with his proviso that persons may freely acquire property only so long as there is 'enough and as good' left for others. (See *Two Treatises of Government*, ed. P. Laslett. 2nd ed. [Cambridge: Cambridge University Press, 1967], Bk. II, Ch. V, Par. 27.) Where there is not enough and as good left for others we presumably have the conditions for an other-regarding communal decision. Locke's proviso has gained new prominence through Nozick's use of it in *Anarchy, State, and Utopia*, pp. 178–182. For a critique of Nozick's position vis-à-vis Locke's proviso, see my 'Nozick, Libertarianism, and Rights'. My thinking on this distinction has also benefited from C. Edwin Baker's discussion of several related distinctions, especially one between 'additive' and 'determinative' conduct. See Baker, 'Counting Preferences in Collective Choice Situations', *UCLA Law Review* 25 (February, 1978), pp. 381–416, esp. pp. 404–408.

CHAPTER SEVEN

1 Feinberg, 'Legal Paternalism', pp. 119–120. See also Tom L. Beauchamp, 'Paternalism and Bio-Behavioral Control', p. 74. For an alternative approach to the problem of slavery contracts, see my 'Mill, Paternalism, and Slavery', *Analysis* 41 (January, 1981), pp. 60–62.

2 Bayles, *Principles of Legislation*, p. 130.

3 See Yale Kamisar, 'Euthanasia Legislation: Some Non-Religious Objections', in *Moral Problems in Medicine*, eds. S. Gorovitz *et al.* (Englewood Cliffs: Prentice-Hall, 1976), pp. 402–414.

4 Cf. Section 2.2.

5 Since this point will have a bearing on many possible applications of the principle of paternalism, it should perhaps be explained more fully. Continuing with the case of the motorcyclist, suppose that at 2 p.m. one Saturday he (call him 'Biker') decides to go riding without his helmet. His friend ('Intervenor') is concerned about the risk and considers trying to force Biker to wear a helmet. Neither Biker nor Intervenor knows at that time whether this or any future ride will result in injuries which the helmet would prevent. Biker's decision to ride without the helmet is encumbered to that extent, although he is aware of this encumbrance. To determine whether intervention is justified, Intervenor must consider whether Biker, if unencumbered, would consent to intervention in these circumstances. Now a fully unencumbered Biker would know whether or not he will ever suffer injuries which could be prevented by helmets. Suppose first that he knows that he will never suffer such injuries. In that instance Biker would

not consent to being forced to wear a helmet in circumstances in which injuries were merely a possibility, for that would be to allow others to override his own judgment about what risks to take, and there would be no gain in doing that. On the other hand, suppose that an unencumbered Biker knows that he will at some point be injured if he does not wear a helmet. In that case he *might* consent to being forced to wear one in circumstances like those at 2 p.m. Saturday, but even here he would have to weigh the benefit of avoiding injuries against the inconvenience of having authorized intervention by others whenever he decides to do something risky. However, at 2 p.m. on Saturday Intervenor cannot know whether Biker will ever be in that kind of accident. Consequently, Intervenor cannot have sufficient evidence that Biker would consent to intervention if unencumbered, and so intervention would be unjustified. Generally, then, a general ignorance of the future never supports paternalistic intervention because intervenors share this sort of encumbrance and thus lack sufficient evidence that their beneficiaries would grant unencumbered consent. Justified paternalism becomes a real possibility only where the beneficiary is encumbered in a way that the intervenor is not.

CHAPTER EIGHT

[1] For a useful discussion of these and other issues relating to the Nazi march in Skokie, see Carl Cohen's articles in *The Nation*: 'Skokie: The Extreme Test of Our Faith in Free Speech', April 15, 1978; 'The Case Against Group Libel', June 24, 1978; and 'Cohen vs. Skokie: An Exchange', May 6, 1978.

[2] The term 'special exclusionary principle' shall be used to refer to any secondary exclusionary principle which states that some specific type of coercive law is open to objections in addition to the coercion objection.

CHAPTER NINE

[1] An act is an act of legal punishment if and only if (1) it imposes something normally considered undesirable, (2) it is imposed for an offense against legal rules, (3) it is imposed on someone declared to be the offender, (4) its imposition is deliberately intended to satisfy conditions (1), (2), and (3), and (5) it is imposed by legal authorities. See, e.g., H. L. A. Hart, 'Prolegomenon to the Principles of Punishment', *Punishment and Responsibility* (New York and Oxford: Oxford University Press, 1968); Stanley I. Benn, 'Punishment', in *Punishment and Rehabilitation*, ed. Jeffrie G. Murphy (Belmont: Wadsworth, 1973), p. 19.

[2] In *Punishment and Rehabilitation*, pp. 40–64.

[3] Morris, 'Persons and Punishment', pp. 42–44, 55–56.

[4] Here and in the discussion to follow, it is assumed that the actual imposition of punishment and the threat of punishment are tied together in that, first, the actual imposition of punishment cannot be justified unless the offender has been threatened and thus warned of the risk of punishment, and, second, some imposition of punishment is in practice necessary to maintain deterrence value associated with the threat of punishment.

[5] John Rawls, 'Legal Obligation and the Duty of Fair Play', in *Law and Philosophy*, ed. Sidney Hook (New York: New York University Press, 1964), pp. 3–18.

[6] See Jeffrie G. Murphy, 'Marxism and Retribution', *Philosophy and Public Affairs* 2 (Spring, 1973), pp. 217–243.

[7] This point is also acknowledged by Rawls in *A Theory of Justice*, pp. 336–337.

[8] See, e.g., Hart, 'Prolegomenon to the Principles of Punishment'; Benn, 'Punishment'; John Rawls, 'Two Concepts of Rules', *Philosophical Review* 64 (1955); pp. 3–32.

[9] This charge is applicable, I believe, to the discussion cited in the preceding note in that they fail to make use of non-utilitarian considerations in defending the institution or practice of punishment or in explaining its general justifying aim. One variant of the standard view which is not subject to this charge is that of Edmund Pincoffs in *The Rationale of Legal Punishment* (New York: Humanities Press, 1966). See esp. Ch. VII.

[10] 'Persons and Punishment'.

[11] Cf. Richard Wasserstrom, 'Why Punish the Guilty?' *Princeton University Magazine* 20 (1964); pp. 14–19; Wasserstrom, 'Punishment', in *Philosophy and Social Issues* (Notre Dame: University of Notre Dame Press, 1980), pp. 132–133; and Jeffrie G. Murphy, 'Marxism and Retribution', p. 219.

[12] Unlike some retributive theories, the present view does not require that we claim that the offender chooses his own punishment; all that is needed is the claim that the offender chooses to *risk* punishment.

[13] One implication of the content condition is that punishment is not justifiable for prohibitions not authorized by the principles of legal coercion *even if they have been enacted through a legitimate political process*. If the political process results in indefensible prohibitions, the most that can be said is that punishment of violators of those prohibitions is excusable.

[14] See Benn, 'Punishment', p. 27.

[15] *Ibid.*, p. 26.

[16] Section 5.4.

[17] Although, of course, it could be a violation in circumstances in which one is responsible for creating the choice between lives.

CHAPTER TEN

[1] Mancur Olson, Jr., *The Logic of Collective Action* (Cambridge: Harvard University Press, 1965), p. 14.

[2] See, e.g., Frank Miller and Rolf Sartorius, 'Population Policy and Public Goods', *Philosophy and Public Affairs* 8 (Winter, 1979); pp. 167–168.

[3] It is of course possible to debate whether a particular good falls under the definition of *public* goods. One could argue, for instance, that parks are not public goods because it would be 'feasible' to deny access to them to those who do not pay; criteria of feasibility would have to be specified to answer this charge. However, for present purposes, the important question is not whether a particular good is a public good, but whether coercion may be used to provide it.

[4] *Social Philosophy*, p. 52.

[5] See *The Report of the Commission on Obscenity and Pornography* (New York: Random House, 1970), pp. 26–32, 169–180; Michael J. Goldstein and Harold S. Kant,

Pornography and Sexual Deviance (Berkeley: University of California Press, 1973), pp. 12–13.

[6] For brevity, I shall focus only on the possibility of a relationship between pornography and rape.

[7] *Report*, p. 32.

[8] *Report*, pp. 469–471, 640–654.

[9] Goldstein and Kant, p. 31.

[10] *Ibid.*, p. 109.

[11] *Report*, p. 179.

[12] Goldstein and Kant, p. 109.

[13] *Report*, p. 457. Emphasis original. See also pp. 614 and 616.

[14] See Feinberg, ' "Harmless Immoralities" and Offensive Nuisances'.

[15] *On Liberty*, Ch. V, Par. 7.

[16] See ' "Harmless Immoralities" and Offensive Nuisances'.

[17] *Ibid.*, p. 102.

[18] *Ibid.*, pp. 102–103.

[19] 'Coercive Restraint of Offensive Actions', *Philosophy and Public Affairs* 8 (Winter, 1979); p. 180.

[20] VanDeVeer points out that condition (2) prevents condition (1) from precluding use of the offense principle where abnormal susceptibilities are involved (*Ibid.*).

[21] ' "Harmless Immoralities" and Offensive Nuisances', p. 103.

[22] *Ibid.*, p. 105.

[23] *Ibid.*, p. 86.

[24] Feinberg, 'Reply to Bayles', in *Issues in Law and Morality*, p. 129.

[25] *Ibid.*, p. 137.

[26] 'Coercive Restraint of Offensive Actions', p. 185.

[27] *Ibid.*, pp. 177–178.

[28] 'Comments: Offensive Conduct and the Law', in *Issues in Law and Morality*, p. 119.

[29] *Ibid.*, p. 120.

[30] 'Reply to Bayles', pp. 137–138.

[31] 'Coercive Restraint of Offensive Actions', pp. 181–182.

[32] I have not, of course, drawn the boundaries of 'invasion of mentation' very sharply; however, as we shall see, doing so is not the solution to the problem of offensive conduct.

[33] 'Reply to Bayles', p. 134.

[34] In a later work, Feinberg abandons the standard of universality as unworkable. See *Rights, Justice, and the Bounds of Liberty* (Princeton, N.J.: Princeton University Press, 1980), p. x.

[35] This is to say that the reformer is on his or her most *defensible* ground in criticizing the views on which laws may be based; this, of course, is not to say that criticizing the views themselves is necessarily the most *effective* way to secure change.

SELECTED BIBLIOGRAPHY

Ackerman, Bruce: 1981, *Social Justice in the Liberal State*, Yale University Press, New Haven.

Acton, H. B. (ed.): 1969, *The Philosophy of Punishment*, Macmillan, London.

Ames, James Barr: 1908, 'Law and Morals', *Harvard Law Review* 22.

Aune, Bruce: 1979, *Kant's Theory of Morals*, Princeton University Press, Princeton, N.J.

Baker, C. Edwin: 1978, 'Counting Preferences in Collective Choice Situations', *UCLA Law Review* 25, pp. 381–416.

Bayles, Michael D.: 1973, 'Comments: Offensive Conduct and the Law', in Care and Trelogan (eds.), *Issues in Law and Morality*, The Press of Case Western Reserve University, London and Cleveland.

Bayles, Michael D.: 1974, 'Criminal Paternalism', in J. R. Pennock and J. W. Chapman (eds.), *Nomos XV: The Limits of Law*, Atherton, Chicago.

Bayles, M. D.: 1976, 'Legislating Morality', *Wayne Law Review* 22, pp. 759–780.

Bayles, Michael D.: 1978, *Principles of Legislation*, Wayne State University Press, Detroit.

Beauchamp, Tom L.: 1977, 'Paternalism and Biobehavioral Control', *The Monist* 60.

Benn, S. I.: 1967, 'Punishment', in Paul Edwards (ed.), *The Encyclopedia of Philosophy*, Vol. 7, Collier-Macmillan, New York.

Benn, S. I.: 1971, 'Privacy, Freedom, and Respect for Persons', in J. R. Pennock and John Chapman (eds.), *Privacy*, Atherton Press, New York.

Berger, Fred R.: 1977, 'Pornography, Sex, and Censorship', *Social Theory and Practice* 4, pp. 183–209.

Berger, Fred R. (ed.): 1980, *Freedom of Expression*, Wadsworth, Belmont, Ca.

Berns, Walter: 1971, 'Pornography vs. Democracy: The Case for Censorship', *Public Interest*, pp. 3–24.

Brown, D. G.: 1972, 'Mill on Liberty and Morality', *Philosophical Review* 81.

Burgh, Richard W.: 1982, 'Do the Guilty Deserve Punishment', *Journal of Philosophy* 79, pp. 193–210.

Carter, Rosemary: 1977, 'Justifying Paternalism', *Canadian Journal of Philosophy* 7.

Clor, Harry M.: 1969, *Obscenity and Public Morality*, University of Chicago Press, Chicago.

Commission on Obscenity and Pornography: 1970, *Report of the Commission on Obscenity and Pornography*, Random House, New York.

Conway, David A.: 1974, 'Law, Liberty and Indecency', *Philosophy* 49.

Cranor, Carl F.: 1979, 'Legal Moralism Reconsidered', *Ethics* 89, pp. 147–164.

Cranor, Carl F.: 1975, 'Toward a Theory of Respect for Persons', *American Philosophical Quarterly* 12.

Darwall, Stephen L.: 1977, 'Two Kinds of Respect', *Ethics* 88.

Dershowitz, Alan: 1974, 'Toward a Jurisprudence of "Harm" Prevention', in J. R.

Pennock and J. W. Chapman (eds.), *The Limits of Law*, Lieber-Atherton, New York.

Devlin, Patrick: 1965, *The Enforcement of Morals*, Oxford University Press, London.

Downie, R. S. and Telfer, Elizabeth: 1970, *Respect for Persons*, Schocken Books, New York.

Dworkin, Gerald: 1971, 'Paternalism', in Richard Wasserstrom (ed.), *Morality and the Law*, Wadsworth, Belmont, Ca. pp. 107–126.

Dworkin, Ronald: 1966, 'Lord Devlin and the Enforcement of Morals', *Yale Law Journal 75*.

Dworkin, Ronald: 1977, *Taking Rights Seriously*, Harvard University Press, Cambridge, Mass.

Feinberg, Joel: 1970, *Doing and Deserving*, Princeton University Press, Princeton, N.J.

Feinberg, Joel: 1971, 'Legal Paternalism', *Canadian Journal of Philosophy* 1, pp. 105–124.

Feinberg, Joel: 1973, *Social Philosophy*, Prentice-Hall, Englewood Cliffs.

Feinberg, Joel: 1973, ' "Harmless Immoralities" and Offensive Nuisances', in Care and Trelogan (eds.), *Issues in Law and Morality*. The Press of Case Western Reserve University, London and Cleveland.

Feinberg, Joel: 1975, 1980, 'Limits to the Free Expression of Opinion', in Joel Feinberg and Hyman Gross (eds.), *Philosophy of Law*, Wadsworth, Belmont, Ca.

Feinberg, Joel: 1977, 'Harm and Self-Interest', in P. M. S. Hacker and J. Raz (eds.), *Law, Morality and Society*, Clarendon Press, Oxford.

Feinberg, Joel: 1979, 'Pornography and the Criminal Law', *University of Pittsburgh Law Review* 40, pp. 567–604.

Feinberg, Joel: 1980, 'Legal Moralism and Freefloating Evils', *Pacific Philosophical Quarterly* 61, pp. 122–155.

Feinberg, Joel: 1980, *Rights, Justice, and the Bounds of Liberty*, Princeton University Press, Princeton, N.J.

Foot, Philippa: 1977, 'Euthanasia', *Philosophy and Public Affairs* 6.

Fotion, N.: 1979, 'Paternalism', *Ethics* 89, pp. 191–198.

Fried, Charles: 1978, *Right and Wrong*, Harvard University Press, Cambridge, Mass.

Gastil, Raymond D.: 1976, 'The Moral Right of the Majority to Restrict Obscenity and Pornography Through Law', *Ethics* 86, p. 231.

Gendin, Sidney: 1970, 'A Plausible Theory of Retribution', *Journal of Value Inquiry* 5.

Gert, Bernard and Culver, Charles: 1976, 'Paternalistic Behavior', *Philosophy and Public Affairs* 6.

Gert, Bernard and Culver, Charles: 1979, 'The Justification of Paternalism', *Ethics* 89, pp. 199–210.

Glover, Jonathan: 1970, *Responsibility*, Humanities Press, New York.

Golding, Martin P.: 1975, *Philosophy of Law*, Prentice-Hall, Englewood Cliffs, N.J.

Goldstein, Michael J. and Kant, Harold S.: 1973, *Pornography and Sexual Deviance*, University of California Press, Berkeley.

Gregor, Mary: 1963, *Laws of Freedom*, Oxford University Press, London.

Gross, Hyman: 1979, *A Theory of Criminal Justice*, Oxford University Press, New York.

Gusfield, Joseph R.: 1968, 'On Legislating Morals: The Symbolic Process of Designating Deviance', *California Law Review 56*.

Gutman, Amy: 1980, 'Children, Paternalism, and Education', *Philosophy and Public Affairs* 9, pp. 338–358.

Haksar, Vinit: 1976, 'Coercive Proposals', *Political Theory* 4, pp. 65–79.

Hare, R. M.: 1963, *Freedom and Reason*, Oxford University Press, London.

Harris, Robert N., Jr.: 1967, 'Private Consensual Adult Behavior: The Requirement of Harm to Others in the Enforcement of Morality', *UCLA Law Review* 14, p. 581.

Hart, H. L. A.: 1955, 'Are There Any Natural Rights?' *Philosophical Review* 64.

Hart, H. L. A.: 1961, 'The Use and Abuse of the Criminal Law', *Oxford Lawyer* 4, p. 7.

Hart, H. L. A.: 1959, 'Immorality and Treason', *Listener* 2, p. 162.

Hart, H. L. A.: 1963, *Law, Liberty, and Morality*, Stanford University Press, Stanford, Ca.

Hart, H. L. A.: 1965, *The Morality of the Criminal Law*, Oxford University Press, London.

Hart, H. L. A.: 1967, 'Social Solidarity and the Enforcement of Morality', *University of Chicago Law Review* 35.

Hart, H. L. A.: 1968, *Punishment and Responsibility*, Oxford University Press, Oxford and New York.

Hayek, F. A. von: 1960, *The Constitution of Liberty*, University of Chicago Press, Chicago.

Henkin, L.: 1963, 'Morals and the Constitution: The Sin of Obscenity', *Columbia Law Review* 63, p. 391.

Hill, Thomas E., Jr.: 1980, 'Humanity as an End in Itself', *Ethics* 91.

Hobhouse, L. T.: 1964, *Liberalism*, Oxford, New York.

Hodson, John D.: 1973, 'Reflections Concerning Violence and the Brain', *Criminal Law Bulletin* 9. Reprinted in Ronald Munson, (ed.), 1979, *Intervention and Reflection: Basic Issues in Medical Ethics*, Wadsworth Publishing Co., Belmont, Ca.

Hodson, John D.: 1977, 'Nozick, Libertarianism, and Rights', *Arizona Law Review* 19, pp. 212–227.

Hodson, John D.: 1977, 'The Principle of Paternalism', *American Philosophical Quarterly* 14, pp. 61–69.

Hodson, John D.: 1978, Review of *Taking Rights Seriously*, by Ronald Dworkin, *Vanderbilt Law Review* 31, pp. 450–471.

Hodson, John D.: 1981, 'Mill, Paternalism, and Slavery', *Analysis* 41, pp. 60–62.

Honderich, Ted: 1969, *Punishment: The Supposed Justifications*, Harcourt, Brace and World, New York.

Honoré, A. M.: 1966, 'Law, Morals and Rescue', in *The Good Samaritan and the Law*, Anchor Books, Garden City.

Hospers, John: 1971, *Libertarianism*, Nash, Los Angeles.

Hughes, Graham: 1962, 'Morals and the Criminal Law', *Yale Law Journal* 71.

Husak, Douglas: 1981, 'Paternalism and Autonomy', *Philosophy and Public Affairs* 10.

Jones, Hardy: 1971, *Kant's Principle of Personality*, University of Wisconsin Press, Madison.

Kant, Immanuel: 1959, *Foundations of the Metaphysics of Morals*, Lewis White Beck (tr.), Bobbs-Merrill, Indianapolis.

Kant, Immanuel: 1964, *The Doctrine of Virtue*, Mary Gregor (tr.), Harper and Row, New York.

Kant, Immanuel: 1970, 'On the Common Saying: That May be True in Theory but It does not Apply in Practice', in H. Reiss (ed.), *Kant's Political Writings*, Cambridge University Press, Cambridge.

Kant, Immanuel: 1965, *The Metaphysical Elements of Justice*, John Ladd (tr.), Bobbs-Merrill, Indianapolis .

Kleinig, John: 1976, 'Good Samaritanism', *Philosophy and Public Affairs* 5, pp. 382–407.

Kleinig, John: 1978, 'Crime and the Concept of Harm', *American Philosophical Quarterly* 15.

Knowles, Dudley R.: 1978, 'A Reformulation of the Harm Principle', *Political Theory* 6, pp. 233–246.

Kristol, Irving: 1971, 'Pornography, Obscenity and the Case for Censorship', *New York Times Magazine* (March 28), p. 24.

Louch, A. R.: 1968, 'Sins and Crimes', *Philosophy* 43. Also in Richard Wasserstrom (ed.), 1971, *Morality and the Law*, Wadsworth, Belmont, Ca.

Maclagan, W. G.: 1960, 'Respect for Persons as a Moral Principle', *Philosophy* 35, Nos. 134 and 135.

Marcuse, Herbert: 1969, 'Repressive Tolerance', in *A Critique of Pure Tolerance*, Beacon Press, Boston.

McCloskey, H. J.: 1965, 'A Non-Utilitarian Approach to Punishment', *Inquiry* 8.

McCloskey, H. J.: 1970, 'Liberty of Expression: Its Grounds and Limits', *Inquiry* 13.

McCloskey, H. J.: 1974, 'Liberalism', *Philosophy* 49, p. 13.

Melden, A. I.: 1978, *Rights and Persons*, University of California Press, Berkeley.

Mewett, A.: 1962, 'Morality and the Criminal Law', *University of Toronto Law Journal* 14.

Mill, John Stuart: 1956, *On Liberty*, Liberal Arts Press, New York.

Mitchell, B.: 1967, *Law, Morality, and Religion in a Secular Society*, Oxford University Press, London.

Monro, D. H.: 1970, 'Liberty of Expression: Its Grounds and Limits (II)', *Inquiry* 13.

Morris, Herbert: 1968, 'Persons and Punishment', *The Monist* 52.

Murphy, Jeffrie G.: 1970, *Kant: The Philosophy of Right*, Macmillan, London.

Murphy, Jeffrie G.: 1971, 'Three Mistakes about Retributivism', *Analysis* 31.

Murphy, Jeffrie G. (ed.): 1973, *Punishment and Rehabilitation*, Wadsworth, Belmont, Ca.

Murphy, Jeffrie G.: 1973, 'Marxism and Retribution', *Philosophy and Public Affairs* 2.

Murphy, Jeffrie G.: 1974, 'Incompetence and Paternalism', *Archiv für Rechts und Sozialphilosophie* 60, pp. 465–486.

Murphy, Jeffrie G.: 1979, *Retribution, Justice, and Therapy*, D. Reidel Publishing Co., Dordrecht, Holland.

Nagel, Ernest: 1975, 'The Enforcement of Morals', in Tom L. Beauchamp (ed.), *Ethics and Public Policy*, Prentice-Hall, Englewood Cliffs.

Note, 1976, 'The Limits of State Intervention: Personal Identity and Ultra-Risky Actions', *Yale Law Journal* 85, pp. 826–846.

Nozick, Robert: 1974, *Anarchy, State, and Utopia*, Basic Books, New York.

Nozick, Robert: 1969, 'Coercion', in Sidney Morgenbesser, Patrick Suppes, and Morton White (eds.), *Philosophy, Science, and Method*, St. Martin's, New York.

Olson, Mancur: 1965, *The Logic of Collective Action*, Harvard University Press, Cambridge, Mass.

Packer, Herbert L.: 1968, *The Limits of the Criminal Sanction*, Stanford University Press, Stanford, Ca.

Paton, H. J.: 1967, *The Categorical Imperative*, Harper and Row, New York.

Peffer, Rodney: 1978, 'A Defense of Rights to Well-Being', *Philosophy and Public Affairs* 8.

Pennock, J. Roland and Chapman, John W. (eds.): 1974, *Nomos XV: The Limits of Law*, Lieber-Atherton, New York.

Pincoffs, Edmund L.: 1966, *The Rationale of Legal Punishment*, Humanities Press, New York.

Powers, William C., Jr.: 1975, 'Autonomy and the Legal Control of Self-Regarding Conduct', *Washington Law Review* 51.

'Principles of Expression and Restriction: A First Amendment Symposium', *University of Pittsburgh Law Review* 40 (Summer, 1979).

Rachels, James: 1975, 'Active and Passive Euthanasia', *New England Journal of Medicine* 292, p. 78.

Radcliff, Peter (ed.): 1966, *Limits of Liberty*, Wadsworth, Belmont, Ca.

Ratcliffe, James M. (ed.): 1966, *The Good Samaritan and the Law*, Anchor Books, Garden City.

Rawls, John: 1971, *A Theory of Justice*, Belknap Press of Harvard University Press, Cambridge, Mass.

Rees, J. C.: 1960, 'A Re-reading of Mill on Liberty', *Political Studies* 8, pp. 113–129.

Reynolds, Noel B.: 1977, 'The Enforcement of Morals and the Rule of Law', *Georgia Law Review* 11.

Richards, David A. J.: 1977, *The Moral Criticism of Law*, Dickenson Publishing Co., Encino and Belmont, Ca.

Rostow, Eugene V.: 1962, 'The Enforcement of Morals', in *The Sovereign Prerogative*, Yale University Press, New Haven.

Russell, Bruce: 1977, 'On the Relative Strictness of Negative and Positive Duties', *American Philosophical Quarterly* 14, pp. 87–97.

Sartorius, Rolf: 1972, 'The Enforcement of Morality', *Yale Law Journal* 81.

Scanlon, Thomas: 1972, 'A Theory of Freedom of Expression', *Philosophy and Public Affairs* 1, pp. 204–226.

Schoeman, Ferdinand: 1976, 'The Enforcement of Matters of Custom and Taste', *Philosophical Studies* 30.

Schwartz, Louis B.: 1963, 'Morals Offenses and the Model Penal Code', *Columbia Law Review* 63.

Shapiro, Michael H.: 1974, 'Legislating the Control of Behavior Control: Autonomy and the Coercive Use of Organic Therapies', *Southern California Law Review* 47, pp. 237–356.

Silverstein, Harry S.: 1974, 'Universality and Treating Persons as Persons', *Journal of Philosophy* 71.

Singer, Peter: 1972, 'Famine, Affluence, and Morality', *Philosophy and Public Affairs* 1, pp. 229–243.

Skolnick, Jerome H.: 1968, 'Coercion to Virtue: The Enforcement of Morals', *Southern California Law Review* 41.

Spelman, Elizabeth V.: 1978, 'On Treating Persons as Persons', *Ethics* 88, pp. 150–161.

Stell, Lance K.: 1979, 'Dueling and the Right to Life', *Ethics* 90, pp. 7–26.

Stephen, James Fitzjames: 1967, *Liberty, Equality, Fraternity*, Cambridge University Press, Cambridge.

Ten, C. L.: 1971, 'Paternalism and Morality', *Ratio* 13, pp. 56–66.

Ten, C. L.: 1980, *Mill on Liberty*, Clarendon Press, Oxford.

Ten, C. L.: 1972, 'Enforcing a Shared Morality', *Ethics* 82, p. 321.

Ten, C. L.: 1968, 'Mill on Self-Regarding Actions', *Philosophy* 63.

Trammell, R. L.: 1975, 'Saving Life and Taking Life', *Journal of Philosophy* 72, p. 131.

VanDeVeer, Donald: 1979, 'Coercive Restraint of Offensive Actions', *Philosophy and Public Affairs* 8.

VanDeVeer, Donald: 1979, 'Paternalism and Subsequent Consent', *Canadian Journal of Philosophy* 9, pp. 631–642.

Wasserstrom, Richard: 1964, 'Why Punish the Guilty?', *Princeton Univerity Magazine* 20.

Wasserstrom, Richard (ed.): 1971, *Morality and the Law*, Wadsworth Publishing Co., Belmont, Ca.

Wasserstrom, Richard: 1980, 'Punishment', in *Philosophy and Social Issues*, University of Notre Dame Press, Notre Dame, Ind.

Wertheimer, Alan: 1977, 'Victimless Crimes', *Ethics* 87.

Wolff, Robert Paul: 1973, *The Autonomy of Reason*, Harper and Row, New York.

Wollheim, Richard: 1959, 'Crime, Sin, and Mr. Justice Devlin', *Encounter* 13, pp. 34–40.

INDEX OF NAMES

INDEX OF SUBJECTS

171

PHILOSOPHICAL STUDIES SERIES
IN PHILOSOPHY

Editors:

WILFRID SELLARS, Univ. of Pittsburgh and KEITH LEHRER, Univ. of Arizona

Board of Consulting Editors:

Jonathan Bennett, Allan Gibbard, Robert Stalnaker, and Robert G. Turnbull

1. JAY F. ROSENBERG, *Linguistic Representation*, 1974.
2. WILFRID SELLARS, *Essays in Philosophy and Its History*, 1974.
3. DICKINSON S. MILLER, *Philosophical Analysis and Human Welfare*. Selected Essays and Chapters from Six Decades. Edited with an Introduction by Lloyd D. Easton, 1975.
4. KEITH LEHRER (ed.), *Analysis and Metaphysics*. Essays in Honor of R. M. Chisholm. 1975.
5. CARL GINET, *Knowledge, Perception, and Memory*, 1975.
6. PETER H. HARE and EDWARD H. MADDEN, *Causing, Perceiving and Believing*. An Examination of the Philosophy of C. J. Ducasse, 1975.
7. HECTOR-NERI CASTAÑEDA, *Thinking and Doing*. The Philosophical Foundations of Institutions, 1975.
8. JOHN L. POLLOCK, *Subjunctive Reasoning*, 1976.
9. BRUCE AUNE, *Reason and Action*, 1977.
10. GEORGE SCHLESINGER, *Religion and Scientific Method*, 1977.
11. YIRMIAHU YOVEL (ed.), *Philosophy of History and Action*. Papers presented at the first Jerusalem Philosophical Encounter, December 1974, 1978.
12. JOSEPH C. PITT, *The Philosophy of Wilfrid Sellars: Queries and Extensions*, 1978.
13. ALVIN I. GOLDMAN and JAEGWON KIM, *Values and Morals*. Essays in Honor of William Frankena, Charles Stevenson, and Richard Brandt, 1978.
14. MICHAEL J. LOUX, *Substance and Attribute*. A Study in Ontology, 1978.
15. ERNEST SOSA (ed.), *The Philosophy of Nicholas Rescher: Discussion and Replies*, 1979.
16. JEFFRIE G. MURPHY, *Retribution, Justice, and Therapy*. Essays in the Philosophy of Law, 1979.
17. GEORGE S. PAPPAS, *Justification and Knowledge: New Studies in Epistemology*, 1979.
18. JAMES W. CORNMAN, *Skepticism, Justification, and Explanation*, 1980.
19. PETER VAN INWAGEN, *Time and Cause*. Essays presented to Richard Taylor, 1980.

20. DONALD NUTE, *Topics in Conditional Logic*, 1980.
21. RISTO HILPINEN (ed.), *Rationality in Science*, 1980.
22. GEORGES DICKER, *Perceptual Knowledge*, 1980.
23. JAY F. ROSENBERG, *One World and Our Knowledge of It*, 1980.
24. KEITH LEHRER and CARL WAGNER, *Rational Consensus in Science and Society*, 1981.
25. DAVID O'CONNOR, *The Metaphysics of G. E. Moore*, 1982.